G000256413

Philip Purser was born in Letchworth Garden City but grew up in more ordinary places. He lives now in Northamptonshire. He is married with three children and one grandchild. For many years he was a television critic with the *Sunday Telegraph*, the old *News Chronicle* and the *Daily Mail* (twice). He has also written novels and screenplays, and published a great deal of miscellaneous fact and fiction, not always distinguishable, as in his most recent novel, *Friedrich Harris: Shooting the Hero* (Quartet Books, 1990). In 1977 he visited Edward James in Ireland and Mexico as part of the research for the former version of this book, *Where Is He Now?* For this new edition he has extensively revised the text to incorporate fresh information and to trace James's life through to its close.

Also by Philip Purser

Poeted
The Final Quest
of Edward James

Philip Purser

QUARTET BOOKS

Revised and enlarged from the original, published as
*Where Is He Now? The Extraordinary Worlds of Edward
James* by Quartet Books 1978

This edition first published by
Quartet Books Limited 1991
A member of the Namara Group
27/29 Goodge Street, London W1P 1FD

British Library Cataloguing in Publication Data
Purser, Philip
  Poeted: the final quest of Edward James.–Rev. ed.
  1. English arts. James, Edward, *1907–1984*
  I. Title   II. Purser, Philip. Where is he now?
  700.92

ISBN 0-7043-0139-3

Typeset by AKM Associates (UK) Ltd, Southall, London
Printed in Great Britain by
Cox & Wyman Ltd, Reading, Berkshire

Acknowledgements

The lines from John Betjeman's *Summoned by Bells* are reproduced by permission of the author's estate and John Murray Ltd; the extract from *The Gardener Who Saw God* by permission of Duckworth & Co. Ltd; that from 'Shut Gates' in *The Bones of My Hand* by permission of the Tragopan Corporation Ltd, which has also given permission for other quotations from Edward James's verse taken from privately printed or circulated editions. The extract from Peter Levi's introduction to *The Heart and the Word* is by permission of Professor Levi and George Weidenfeld & Nicolson Ltd. The author is indebted, for their help, to Lady Menuhin, Mrs Diana Beresford, Mr Angus James, the Hon. Desmond Guinness, and others of Edward's friends and relations; at West Dean, to Mr M. Heymann, FRICS, agent, Mr Peter Sarginson, principal of West Dean College, and Miss Sharon Kusunoki, archivist; in America to Mr and Mrs Avery Danziger, Dr A. M. Koller, Dr William Emboden and, once again, Mr and Mrs Gustave Field.

Introduction

In the summer of 1945 two men were travelling in Mexico with packs and sleeping bags piled in the back of the car. It was at that pause in history when the war in Europe was over but a long slog, everyone thought, still lay ahead against Japan. The two had driven down through New Mexico as unconscious as the rest of the world of the awesome weapon being assembled in the desert there. The news of Hiroshima, and then of Nagasaki, was to break in a few days' time. For the moment, as they followed a rough road into the eastern Sierra Madre, the war, and indeed the whole civilization at stake in the war, seemed absurdly remote. The sky was an intense blue; on each side of the road was jungle; ahead, the peaks beckoned. They crossed the Río Santa María by primitive ferry and on the bank of one of its tributaries stopped for a swim.

One of the men was a sergeant in the US Army, a good-looking, cheerful Texan with Indian blood. For him the impact of Mexico was – or should have been – total, because he was on leave after two years in the Aleutians, foggy sub-arctic islands whose name alone was enough to signify an unenviable posting in the songs and radio shows of the day, and he had hardly seen the sun in that time, let alone sweltered in its heat. His companion was short and smooth-skinned, looking much younger than his age, which was nearly thirty-eight. He was the driving force of the expedition; it was his car, his money, his pursuit of the romantic and the exotic which determined their wanderings – just now, into the mountains in search of wild orchids said to run riot in the valley below a curious hook-shaped peak called Huestmolotepl.

He was, of course, Edward James, and in a sense this journey was a model of his whole life until then, full of enthusiasms, yearnings and passionate attachments that were never quite fulfilled. Even his relationship with the Texan, Roland McKenzie, was under a certain strain. Their sensibilities were too different. Just as distant clouds had parted to give a first glimpse of Huestmolotepl like a cocked thumb on the skyline, the soldier had destroyed the moment for James by blowing cigarette smoke, for God's sake, across his face.

By the river now, though, it was idyllic enough. Edward was sunning himself after his swim. McKenzie came out of the water, naked, grinning. On the bank was a big patch of bright blue and yellow flowers. He jumped into the middle of it, and the flowers exploded into the air. They were giant butterflies. They wheeled and swirled and as they began to settle again did an extraordinary thing: attracted perhaps by the smell of wet flesh they settled on the Texan until he was clothed in

2

butterflies, like a cheerful, clowning Mayan God. The vision remained imprinted on the mind of Edward James as the one perfect realization – or surrealization – of something that he sought all his life.

If you were born extremely rich but uninterested in power or making more money, what was to drive you on? If nevertheless you wrote or drew or composed, nothing much less than genius would get you taken seriously – the rich man's well-advertised difficulty in gaining the Kingdom of Heaven was child's play by the side of his trying to make the Republic of Letters. If you displayed an undeniable flair for being right about pictures, and the pictures you spotted were surrealist, how tempting to take refuge in the surrealist belief that art was the product of accident, and the artist merely the one who could recognize beauty and magic when they were offered.

James flitted in and out of the fringes of history for half a century while remaining curiously unknown, considering that he spurred on such painters as Dalí, Magritte and Tchelitchew, inspired a ballet by Brecht and Weill, was married to (and luridly divorced from) one of the most beautiful women in Europe, lived for years in Hollywood, amassed a definitive art collection, endowed a college and was quite possibly the Queen of England's bastard great-uncle. He is the model for two of Magritte's most celebrated paintings and also for one head of the two-headed man – the other is the artist's own – in Tchelitchew's enormous canvas *Phenomena* in Moscow.

3

He pops up in memoirs along the Biography & Memoirs shelf from 'Acton, Harold', to 'Zorina, Vera', but was never in *Who's Who*. The spotlight would pick him out briefly, then he would vanish again into mysterious exile. John Betjeman, who owed the first publication of his verse to James, asked in his autobiographical *Summoned by Bells*, 'But where's he now? What does he do?'

In the first version of this book, published in 1978 under the title *Where Is He Now?*, I was able to answer that James was back in Mexico, and what he was doing was trying to re-create, literally and astonishingly in concrete terms, that vision of butterflies. What may be his more enduring monument, I can now add, was going ahead prosaically in rural Sussex. What he himself wanted most to be remembered for was secreted around the world in suitcases and boxes and bundles of letters and store-rooms full of expensive, uncut, never-distributed volumes of verse.

1

The Court Circular for 19 November 1906 reported that the king had left the palace that afternoon for West Dean Park, Chichester, to honour Mr and Mrs W. James with a visit. Edward Frank Willis James was born exactly nine months later on 16 August 1907, thus lending arithmetical support to the widely held belief that he was the illegitimate son of Edward VII. Certainly that gamey old monarch was very fond of Mrs James, and, at a time when it was unusual for a king to lodge with a commoner, stayed frequently at West Dean Park. It is also a fact that he stood as the boy's godfather, and presented him with a gold goblet bearing his name. In later life Edward James was supposed to bear some resemblance to old Teddy. But he always maintained that his small stature, small features and aquiline nose were much more characteristic of the James family, and of Willie James in particular. Besides, the king never came to West Dean alone; if he wasn't accompanied by Queen Alexandra he brought Mrs Keppel, his accepted mistress; under either circumstance any philandering would have been out of the question.

Nor was Willie James the kind of man to accept the role of *mari complaisant.*

Edward had his own, more romantic explanation of the king's visits. He was not the lover of Mrs Willie, née Evelyn Forbes. He was her father! Evelyn's mother, who married the Scottish baronet, Sir Charles Forbes of Newe, had been brought up on an estate bordering the royal estate at Balmoral. What likelier happening than a little hanky-panky in the heather, some time around 1865, with a younger and notoriously sprightly Prince of Wales? Edward claimed to have a bundle of royal letters left to him by his mother that proved it. When discovered among his papers after his death, unfortunately, they failed to confirm this version of his lineage. Members of the family remain convinced that Mrs Willie did have an affair with the king. Certainly there was a very rum story, retailed by Edward himself, of her dressing herself as a clockwork doll, complete with key and painted face, and being borne into the royal presence in an enormous cardboard box lined with tissue. When the king opened it, she emerged with jerky mechanical movements to dance for him, which doesn't sound altogether a daughterly gesture.

Whatever the truth, Edward was firmly accepted by Willie James as his heir. The family, originally English or, as Edward preferred, Irish, had been settled in America since the eighteenth century. Henry James and his brother William, the philosopher, were cousins of Mr Willie's. The James riches came at first from timber – Edward's great-grandfather bought up vast tracts of woodland in New York State, and Edward used to say that his own passion for planting trees must have come from some instinct to redress his ancestor's wholesale felling. This man's son, Daniel James, is the key figure in subsequent genealogy. He married first into the Phelps family, thereby adding rich mining interests to the timber. Leaving the children of this marriage in America to continue the American branch of the family, he re-migrated to England in 1847 with his second bride, Sophia Hitchcock, to set up what became the English branch. He settled at Woolton, near Liverpool, handy for the transatlantic steamers by which he maintained control of his business, and had three sons. Frank grew up to be an explorer and big-game hunter, duly killed by an elephant. Arthur was a well-known racehorse owner with a country seat at Coton, near Rugby, and a town house in Grafton Street which had one of the first private lifts in London. When the guest of honour fell down the shaft and was found dead, Mrs Arthur – Edward's Aunt Venetia – ruled that the dinner party should nevertheless go ahead, with the other guests being told that he had been unavoidably detained. William Dodge James, always known as Willie, was content to be described as a landowner. He had acquired West Dean Park in 1890, from a Mr Bower who had bought it from the Peachey family, the earls of Selsey. It comprised 10,000 acres of Sussex downland north of Chichester, many farms and the house itself, which dated originally from

Elizabethan times but had been greatly extended and 'gothicized' by James Wyatt about 1790, with a flinty grey façade and mock battlements.

Photographs of Willie James show a handsome, rather ordinary face. He wore a heavy moustache and brushed his hair back from a lofty brow. He had also been something of a traveller and sportsman before he married. With Frank he journeyed to Afghanistan, Abyssinia, Somaliland and the Sudan. In his yacht *Lancashire Witch*, he cruised arctic waters. His prowess as a shot, not to mention the acres of shooting now at his disposal, provided the enduring basis for his friendship with Edward VII. The West Dean visitors' book would be spattered with the signatures of royalty and little drawings by Mrs Willie of dead pheasants raining from the sky. Not even a gaffe by the wife of an American cousin seems to have done any harm. As the king went out with a gun, she wished him, 'Good hunting, Your Majesty!'

Mrs Willie gave birth to four daughters over a period of years: Millicent; Alexandra, always known as Xandra; Sylvia; and finally Audrey. Edward would sooner or later tell you she was the illegitimate one of the brood, the fruit of a Russian escapade of Mrs Willie's with Sir Edward Grey, later Lord Grey of Falloden and author of a famously doomy remark on the eve of the First World War: 'The lamps are going out all over Europe; we shall not see them lit again in our lifetime.' The occasion was supposed to have been the coronation of Tsar Nicholas II in St Petersburg, which Mr and Mrs Willie attended as members of the Prince of Wales's entourage. As foreign secretary, Grey would presumably have been there too – only Edward James could have satisfied himself in the matter of his sister's paternity on the strength of a 'presumably'. Unfortunately for his thesis, this event preceded Audrey's arrival in the world by four years. Anyway, the family now seemed complete. There were no further children for seven years. Then, to everyone's surprise, and the chagrin of some, Edward arrived.

He was born into a world of luxury, leisure and the ever-attendance of servants that even the costume serials on television have never fully evoked. Twelve footmen were on duty at West Dean, dressed in mulberry coloured livery over striped black and yellow waistcoats. Their buttons were embossed with the James coat-of-arms. Mrs Willie had her personal footman whose only duty was to hand her anything she wanted and pick up anything she dropped. The children were brought up by nannies and governesses. When once the Kaiser came to visit, said Edward, the French governess turned her back and the German governess swooned. When, another time, Mrs Willie sent for a child to accompany her to church and was asked which one, she is supposed to have snapped, 'How should I know? Whichever one goes with my blue gown.' She was dressed by Worth, and Edward said that in an age of not particularly becoming fashions, she always managed to look beautiful. He remembered oyster silks, high chokers of pearls, little bunches of

Parma violets pinned to furs, and the letters she was constantly writing in blue ink on blue paper to her friends and relatives and gossips.

The seasons of the year were marked by stately progresses from West Dean to the town house in Bryanston Square and thence to Greywalls, on the Firth of Forth, near Edinburgh, where the late summer would be spent and where Edward, as it happened, was born. His homecoming to West Dean at the age of two months was the occasion for a grand ceremony with fireworks and music. It was also at Greywalls that Edward claims to have registered his first interest in art, at the age of three. They'd been visiting Lord and Lady Wemyss at Gosford and everyone had admired a Botticelli of the infant Jesus that was the pride of the Wemyss collection. Next day Edward was found by his nurse lying in a curious position. 'Master Edward, what are you doing?' 'I'm being a bottled cherry.'

From the same Scottish summers Edward would, in later days, date, not altogether fancifully, the exercise of his imagination that was to make him a surrealist. He was forced to struggle against prosaic nanny replies to his infant speculations. An instance he never forgot was when he wondered what would happen if he shot an arrow straight up into the sky. Would it come back and hit him in the head? 'Master Edward, you shouldn't ask such things. It's not nice.' And, sent early to bed every evening because he was thought to be a delicate child, he would lie awake listening to the surf and the seabirds until, in frustration, he turned his cot into a flying castle, a palace under the sea, a tower rising up through trees. 'I was compelled to invent fantasies,' he told me, 'just to avoid going mad in bed!'

These very early years – rather touchingly, since he can't have remembered very much from them – became the golden years in Edward's estimation. For when he was only five his father died after being taken ill on a trip to South Africa, and the prison-house shades closed in. The family was in London at the time. Edward was packed off to stay with a bleak old kinsman, Lord Wolverton. He remembered sobbing and sobbing when told he would never see his father again. Worse, from his grief his mother suddenly realized that she occupied no comparable position in his affections; he was much fonder of his nurse than his Mama. The nurse was dismissed. It was, Edward would say, a double bereavement.

Willie James's bronze effigy, by Goscombe John, lies in West Dean church. He could be a crusader knight of old, except for the bronze moustache, the deputy lieutenant's uniform with neatly pressed trousers, the insignia of a Companion of the Royal Victorian Order at his neck and the one Jubilee and two Coronation medals meticulously reproduced on his breast.

2

The estate that Edward inherited from his father –
or would inherit when he was twenty-five – turned
out to consist, rather literally, of the West Dean
estate. Though Willie Dodge James had been an
extremely wealthy man, the wealth was tied up
either in his property in Britain or in stocks in the
United States. To the timber and mining interests
old Daniel had added a massive investment in the
railways as they opened up the continent, and the
family now owned something like a seventh of the
entire American railroad system. What wasn't to
hand was ready cash, and the death duties lately
introduced by Lloyd George were unfortunately
required – at that time – to be paid in cash. So
much railway stock had to be sold at once that its
value dipped. After the provision of £8,000 a year
to the widow (who remarried quite shortly),
settlements in trust of £120,000 on the eldest
daughter and of £100,000 on each of the other
three, Edward was left with only a few hundred a
year and the upkeep of those sprawling, costly
acres. At least, that is how Edward always viewed
his lot. He had never felt much love for his sisters,

believing them – with some justification, perhaps – to have resented his late intrusion into their expectations. Now he grew up convincing himself that they had taken his patrimony while leaving him all the bills to pay. Certainly the house at West Dean had to be let within a year or two, and this arrangement would itself become another of the grievances which Edward aired for the rest of his life, accusing his trustees – or rather, a particular trustee, his much older brother-in-law Henry Howard – of having let the place at a peppercorn rent for his own dishonourable ends. In due course some outlying parts of the estate had also to be sold to pay for Edward's education. Meanwhile he was still a rich child, if no longer the heir to buoyant, self-renewing billions. When he was twenty-one he would come into his late Uncle Frank's money (that was the one killed by an elephant), and be a millionaire or as close to it as dammit.

Mrs Willie, or Evie as she was known to friends and relations, married again when Edward was six. Her new husband was Colonel 'Dozy' Brinton, a Guards officer; the decision to leave West Dean may have owed something to the outbreak of war in 1914, when the colonel went with his regiment to France. Edward claimed characteristically that he was not a very brave soldier and soon came back to London as a staff officer. He was an extremely handsome man, a ladies' man, and although Edward always spoke disparagingly of him, seems to have been a fond stepfather. It was assumed that he had been Evie's lover for a long time; I have even heard from one cousin the lingering suspicion that Dozy, rather than either Edward VII or Willie James, may have been Edward's true father.

Edward, it has to be said, displayed no greater affection for his mother. The picture he painted of her from his childhood was hardly flattering. The doll-like prettiness was becoming exaggerated by a thyroid deficiency that gave her protuberant eyes. At West Dean she had continued to live in grand style while suffering premonitions of revolution, and would descend on cottagers with calves-foot jelly and cast-off clothes in the vague hope of ensuring her own immunity. But her wartime endeavours, Edward conceded, were above reproach. If a good cause attracted her attention, she was a brilliant and tireless organizer. She raised the money for, and ran, two hospitals for troops with facial injuries, then a scheme to provide lodgings for officers' widows, whose pensions – she had discovered – often took months to come through.

She was also, all her life, a fine needlewoman who would embroider the curtains for her various houses. In London they had now moved from Bryanston Square to No. 35 Wimpole Street, an early nineteenth century house of no special distinction. Edward always rather liked it, if only from romantic associations. Just across the street was No. 50, where Elizabeth Barrett had been cooped up until rescued by Robert Browning. When Edward was ill once, he watched through his bedroom window as the Barrett house was

14

torn apart to be turned into flats, and saw exposed, before it was scraped off, the wallpaper she must have stared at, even the shadowy outline of her bed-head.

Edward started school, first at a day establishment in Orchard Street. A year later, following the barbaric custom of the ruling classes, he was packed off to prep school at the age of nine. Evie had picked the school on snobbish rather than practical grounds, such as hygiene. She preferred to believe that bodily functions did not exist, Edward used to say. The school had eight lavatories for eighty boys and allowed only ten minutes between breakfast and the first lesson. With some further assistance from the school diet, Edward became chronically constipated. His mother overreacted during the holidays and called in a surgeon who, like the Harley Street smoothies in Shaw's *The Doctor's Dilemma*, had lately developed his private speciality. At the age of twelve Edward lost a length of his intestine in the first of the many operations to which his abdomen would bear witness.

Eton he liked little better; the lessons bored him and he learned more from his schoolfellows, he claimed, in particular a boy called John Lawrence (subsequently Sir John, the linguist and Russian scholar) who had read all Dostoyevsky and had an enthusiasm for Renaissance art. Harold Acton was also in Edward's house, but Edward found his brand of aestheticism too cloying. As a solitary boy growing up at West Dean, he had spent his days outdoors whenever he could. In particular he loved the arboretum, originally planted by the Selseys and augmented by Willie James with trees brought back from his travels. He was still a country landowner's son who enjoyed hunting and was a good shot, though already beginning to dislike the idea of taking life. At the age of fifteen he wrote a poem, 'Lines Written on the Butt of My Gun', lamenting the need to kill in order to live. His mother found it for she allowed no privacy – not even a lock on the bathroom door – and when he retrieved it much later she had noted in the margin, 'Very morbid. Must show to Florrie Bridges,' Florrie Bridges being a neighbour and confidante and wife of a no-nonsense general.

Evie's reluctance to acknowledge the facts of digestion extended to other facts of life. Edward said his sisters knew so little about sex they all had alarming wedding nights. A similar lack of imagination on her part helped to bring about the incident which gave him a certain boyhood notoriety – Tom Driberg did not fail to attach it to the reference to Edward in his memoirs, themselves notorious, published under the title *Ruling Passions.* A Liberal politician called Lord Harcourt who was a friend of the family apparently had a weakness for young boys. Edward kept his distance, but after he and his mother had stayed at his country house one weekend, and were about to leave on the Monday morning, she insisted that he go up and thank their host in his bedroom. Edward descended again hurriedly and on the verge of tears. In the motor car going home, she scolded him for his lack of politeness until finally he blurted out the truth. His lordship had exposed himself.

That evening, says Edward, Evie donned a dressing gown, hid her hair in a silk cap and arranged herself in a suitably grave pose in order to deliver a solemn warning against the dangers of evil men, whom she listed as Nero, Heliogabalus, Benvenuto Cellini – who had actually proclaimed the offence in writing! – Oscar Wilde and now Lord Harcourt. She also complained so loudly about him to her friends that the luckless man was disgraced, and eventually met his death in circumstances calling for an inquest. The jury recorded a verdict of misadventure.

When Edward was sixteen or seventeen Evie sold the house at Gullane, Greywalls, where he had been born and where he had lain in bed listening to the sea. The better news was that for the last two years of his schooling he was being allowed to escape to the more agreeable surroundings of La Rosée, an expensive private establishment in Switzerland. His mother had misgivings at first, but was won over, Edward said, when she discovered that his room-mate was a German princeling. Oxford loomed pleasurably ahead.

3

Charting his upward progress through under-graduate society in *Summoned by Bells*, John Betjeman confesses:

> Week after sunny week
> I climbed, still keeping in, I thought, with God,
> Until I reached what seemed to me the peak –
> The leisured set in Canterbury Quad.

Canterbury Quad is, or was, the richest precinct of the richest Oxford college, Christ Church. Originally it was a college in its own right, for Benedictine scholars from Canterbury. The present buildings date from the same period as West Dean House, indeed were built by the same architect, Wyatt, which should have helped Edward James feel at home when he arrived to join its leisured set of the Michaelmas term of 1926. He was given a set of rooms handsome even by Canterbury Quad standards; four of them instead of the usual two, and overlooking the Dean's garden. He moved in in style. The dining room was hung with Flemish tapestries, the bedroom with crimson, grey and silver silk. A little extra room he had papered in a Napoleonic design of gold bees on a white ground, and the Oxford upholsterer who made the curtains was horrified at Edward's insistence they should reach the floor and not merely the sills. The large drawing room – ah, the drawing room – was given a purple ceiling and a frieze in gold lettering on black, ARS LONGA VITA BREVIS SED VITA LONGA SI SCIAS UTI, which Edward rashly attributed to Seneca and that may be roughly translated as, 'Art is long, life is short, but you can make life seem longer if you know how to use it.'

Tom Driberg, a Christ Church contemporary (others included Christopher Sykes, Quintin Hogg, Valentine Dyall, Adam Black, Harry Oppenheimer, W.H. Auden and William Acton, Harold's young brother), remembered most vividly the 'latest French and American music belching from the mouths of busts of Roman emperors'. Betjeman, himself at Magdalen, celebrates in his poem the breakfasts of champagne and Virginia ham, the heady talk of Eliot and Wilde and Sachie's (Sacheverell Sitwell's) *Southern Baroque Art*, and each reciting to the other his latest poem while outside, in the rain, pale and uninteresting undergraduates trudged to lectures and tutorials.

This picture of perfumed indolence is not altogether complete. Reading history his first year under E. F. Jacob, a noted medievalist, Edward satisfactorily passed history prelim. In his second year he switched to modern languages with Frank Taylor, a New Zealander, as his tutor and every expectation of gaining a reasonable degree. He rode to hounds with the Bicester, buzzed up to London for the evening to see the ballet, and discovered an interest in printing. His closest friends were neither hearties nor aesthetes but social equals such as Basil Ava, heir to the Marquess of Dufferin, Lord Birkenhead's son Viscount Furneaux and – when he came up – Randolph Churchill. He had already met the Churchills through Professor Lindemann, who was a friend of his mother and a crony of Winston Churchill, destined to become the future war leader's scientific adviser. Edward remembered Lindemann telling him, as early as 1927, how atomic physics would lead one day to an atomic bomb.

But there is no doubt that he made his the most conspicuous wealth among a wealthy set.* When

---

* Oxford's millionaire undergraduates towards the end of the 1920s were paraded by the late Maurice Richardson in the course of a famous dissertation in *The Times Literary Supplement* that eventually applied itself to reviewing the original version of this book. They included Jock Whitney, Bill Astor, Alfred Duggan and William Acton, 'who if not precisely a millionaire, behaved madly like one. . . riding in point-to-points and giving immensely lavish parties at which the servants would stagger in with hip-baths full of lobsters'. Evan Morgan (Lord Tredegar), though no longer up at the university, still haunted Oxford at the weekends, throwing fancy-dress parties at the Randolph and airing the same passion for seedy pet birds as Edward was later to acquire. Richardson remembered Morgan buying a parakeet in Thame market that he trained to creep up his trouser leg and poke its head out through his fly-buttons. 'The effect on old ladies can be imagined.'

20

Ava asked to borrow his car, Edward *gave* it to him and bought another. If one was looking for the most extravagant social change of Edward's lifetime, it would be not the decline of the great houses but the sheer unthinkability, these days, of a privileged class of gentlemen-commoners owing their place at university openly to wealth and snobbery. This is not to say that the comparably privileged do not exist; merely that they no longer advertise the fact. I visited Edward's old rooms a few years ago, still identified by the rubric Canterbury 3–3. They were shared and shabby and anonymous, succeeding students leaving only a poster or a plastic cup or a fresh burn on the carpet as evidence of their occupancy; even the view of the Dean's Garden that Edward enjoyed was now bisected by a new building, ironically (in the light of Edward's later renown as a collector) a picture gallery.

According to all accounts of Oxford at this time, homosexuality was professed or pretended by many, if not most, of its *jeunesse dorée*. Whether this stemmed from fashionable affectation or a boarding school education is hard to say, but either way Edward's own inclinations – which will be discussed again – would have seemed to fit in well enough. He confided to John Betjeman's biographer, Bevis Hillier, that he was attracted by the young John despite his greenish, sticky-out teeth.

In his second year Betjeman persuaded him to come to the rescue of the undergraduate newspaper *Cherwell*, which was in financial trouble. He succeeded Betjeman as its editor, and designed a new cover for it. Characteristically, he soon tired of this chore, but from it came his later and more important publishing collaboration with the poet. Both their Oxford sojourns, as it happened, were coming to an end. Betjeman was first rusticated, then sent down, for persistently failing the compulsory divinity exam. Edward's departure was less heroic. Christ Church records indicate no more than that he was late back to college for the last two of the six terms he kept. His own explanation of his decision not to continue is that he enjoyed a reputation at Oxford for being brilliant but knew that he wouldn't be able to sustain it in his final exams.

There were other factors, as always with Edward James rather hard to arrange in order of relevance, and sometimes contradictory. In the memoirs he recorded for George Melly (*Swans Reflecting Elephants*, 1982) he told Melly that he had already fallen in love with Tilly Losch and wanted to be in London, where she was appearing in revue. He told me, only a few days later, that he was tired of preparing for life and wanted to play some real part in the world. He had been to stay with Harold Nicolson and Vita (Sackwille-West) in Berlin, where Harold was counsellor at the British Embassy. His distant cousin and Christ Church contemporary, Christopher Sykes, was also there, having secured an appointment as honorary attaché. It all seemed very exciting and important. Edward immediately set out to engineer the same sort of thing for himself.

In fact, this visit can't have occurred until Edward had already left Oxford, and his own little diplomatic appointment came a year later. In all probability it was family fortunes which most distracted him when he should have been about to return to the university for his third and last year, literally so in the case of his late Uncle Frank's money, into which he came on his twenty-first birthday in August 1928. He was now an extremely wealthy young man.

Then there was his mother. Evie had divorced Colonel Brinton on grounds of adultery. She was in her sixties, suffering from heart trouble and gall-stones. Though she retained the house in Wimpole Street, she was spending more and more time in the South of France. Edward stayed with her as often as he could, mainly – he used to say – because no one else would. She had a knack of finding anyone's vulnerable spot and needling away at it; she lost friends and found it hard to keep personal servants. He, for his part, was becoming irritable and suspicious, especially when his money was involved.

Evie asked him to build her a house on the Riviera. Edward agreed. The difficulty was that she wanted a level plot so that she might walk in the garden without exertion, while insisting on Roquebrune, where the land rose steeply from the sea. Fifty years later Edward would still grumble, as sourly as if it had happened only yesterday, at the extortionate price he had been forced to pay. In the end, he said he spent £100,000 on a property he could sell for only a tenth of the sum – for in

May 1929, with the house barely finished, Evie Brinton died at the age of sixty-three following an operation for the removal of gall-stones.

She left her money to the four daughters. The son was to have the house in Wimpole Street and the villa at Roquebrune. Edward's grief, never very pronounced, evaporated altogether when he discovered what this property was going to cost him in unpaid bills, French estate duties and all the other expensive complications which invariably attended his transactions.

There were also medical and funeral bills and many other debts Evie had run up, including large sums owed to her stockbroker. Rightly or wrongly, the rest of the family expected Edward to shoulder the burden alone – an imposition he later adapted for the hero of his novel *The Gardener Who Saw God*. There were continuing suspicions of West Dean being let at too low a rent, or grumbles about improvements to the house authorized by the trustees before he came of age. Distrust began to poison every activity, every new enthusiasm, into which Edward propelled himself. His cook in Rome in 1930 would cheat him over the food bills, his cook in Hollywood twenty years later would do the same. If he sent a picture to be cleaned, the restorer was a zealot who ruined it. If he invited a composer into his house to write a great symphony, the composer and the composer's wife would be forever in Harrods ordering goodies on his account. If he struck a deal with a painter to paint a fresco, the painter would eat his food and drink his drink but never complete the fresco. If he wanted to buy a house, word would somehow get around that he was who he was, and overnight the price would double.

Year by year he accumulated the peevish repertoire of stories of being cheated and robbed and taken for granted which he would rehearse in wearisome detail for the rest of his life. It was like having to listen to a hypochondriac's medical history. Yet to have been gulled so often he must have been – and sometimes obviously was – generous and impulsive and rather innocent.

His mother's death brought him an invitation to visit his immensely rich American uncle, Arthur Curtis James, and his Aunt Harriet. Edward had an enjoyable stay in New York, including a silly escapade in which he stole a sandhill crane, a very large bird, from the Bronx Zoo. This became one of the elaborate anecdotes that could be almost as hard to take as the complaints. On his return to England he learned that his Aunt Venetia had procured for him the honorary attachment, at a foreign embassy, that he had been seeking.

4

Edward went to Rome to play at affairs of state. Just as Canterbury Quad's architecture must have made him feel at home, so now the role of honorary attaché should have seemed a logical continuation of life as a gentleman-commoner at Christ Church. If you didn't actually pay for the privilege of being a gentleman diplomat you certainly didn't receive a salary. On the other hand, it was not done to be too ostentatious a spender and thus embarrass the career diplomats. The first of three mistakes Edward made, he believed, was to arrive with a chauffeur-driven Rolls-Royce, though the ambassador's displeasure (he was Sir Ronald Graham) did not inhibit him from deploying Edward, and the Rolls, and its chauffeur, if some distinguished visitor had to be met at the railway station. Edward also rented not one but two fourteenth-century palaces in which to live: the Palazzo Celesia and the Palazzo Orsini, facing each other across the Tiber with a little island between and a bridge linking all three. Sometimes guests would be invited to take dinner in one palace and stroll across for coffee in the other, where a string quartet played.

The cook had come off the liner *Rex* and had to be discouraged from a taste that still ran to such scenic effects as lobster with eyes lit by electricity or an ice confection in the shape of the Victor Emmanuel Memorial. He also failed to take care of the crates of sugar which Edward had ordered from Fortnum & Mason before he left because his sister Sylvia had assured him, wrongly, that sugar was not to be found in Italy, so that rats got into it and one day Edward came home from his dipomacy to find the façade of the Orsini Palace whitened as by a miraculous snowfall. The cook had been tipping sugar into the street from an upper window, and lodging in the carvings and pinnacles, it glistened in the sun. Rain came in the night to wash it away, but life was sweet enough already. For the hot summer Edward added a villa on the Aventine to his establishment. The Rolls was supplemented by a racy Alfa-Romeo. There was a companion he was evidently fond of, Francesco. One day they drove into the *campagna* and filled the car with baskets of wild narcissi bought cheap from a farmer, and remembering to give half of them to Lady Graham for the embassy, Edward even managed to ingratiate himself there. Alas, two further contretemps with Sir Ronald lay in wait.

The first occurred while the ambassador was away on leave. Edward was an animal-lover from childhood. He was upset by the narrow cages in which the live eagle and the live she-wolf, ancient emblems and mascots of Rome, were confined on

27

Palatine Hill. He borrowed a sheet of ambassadorial writing paper to address a letter to the authorities, pointing out what an unfortunate impression this gave visitors from England, and would it not be a truer reflection of Signor Mussolini's enlightened administration if the creatures could be given premises more like the Mappin Terraces in the London Zoo? Mr James would attend to any reply.

Edward was summoned to the Palazzo Venezia, at Mussolini's decree, he believed, but his youth disconcerted the officials who met him and the nearest he got to the dictator was an outer office. He said his piece and was politely rebuffed. Months later, to his gratification, it was announced that as a consequence of Il Duce's well-known humanity and love for all species, new quarters were to be built for the wolf and the eagle. Unfortunately Sir Ronald found out about the letter.

The second incident was more serious, both by Foreign Service standards and as an early illustration of the petulance Edward allowed to diminish so many of the activities to which he brought his energy. He was on duty at the embassy one languid Sunday. Intelligence came in from a correspondent to the effect that, against the provisions of the Locarno Treaty limiting naval construction, the keels of three warships appeared to have been laid down at La Spezia. It was Edward's task to encode the message and relay it to London. It was hot. The flies bothered him. The combination locks on the safe containing the code

28

books eluded his skill until his fingers ached. Finally he got the safe open, whizzed off a signal and went home. In his hurry he converted three keels into three hundred, aroused alarm in the Foreign Office and brought poor Ramsay Mac-Donald, the prime minister, hurrying back to Downing Street from Chequers. The ambassador sent him on leave. For the rest of his life Edward used to maintain that he was still only on leave, and could in theory be recalled at any time. In dreary fact the *Foreign Office List* recorded his resignation as of 12 October 1930.

5

It wasn't the best of times for most people, as the frenzied 1920s subsided into the depressed 1930s, but London life, meaning the life of a favoured square mile or so in its centre, went on much as ever. In the grand town houses as many servants were kept as in Edwardian days. The débutante seasons continued unflaggingly. Rather opulent nightclubs opened. Young explorers off to Greenland or Spitsbergen danced their last evening away in the fashionable new May Fair Hotel. Back from Rome, Edward resumed the life he had been marking out for himself on the edge of this society.

He was too much a product of his upbringing to be able to escape it altogether. He loved going out, he could never resist a party, he was careful not to offend the matriarchs who supervised the social scene. At the same time he acquired a certain reputation for candour. 'The trouble with you, Edward,' the formidable Lady Cunard said to him. 'is that you will go around telling the truth. Now society is based upon a lie' – telling the story, he would imitate her piping voice with a protracted 'li-i-ie' – 'and if you persist you will not be received in decent houses!'

Not that Edward's own house at 35 Wimpole Street, on the wrong side of Oxford Street, was quite the address that might have been expected of a wealthy young man about town. Mayfair was the accepted quarter. But then, Edward was never anxious to be regarded as a man about town. What he wanted to be most was a writer or artist or publisher or editor. He cultivated the company of artists without realizing, at first, that they needed to work in order to eat. He told a story against himself of how he was always hanging around Rex Whistler's studio in Fitzroy Street ('He was very poor, you know'), tremendously impressed by Whistler's refusal to answer the telephone when he was at his drawing board, but unable to see that his presence was just as much a distraction. The artist was too modest to tell him so, and in the end Oliver Messel had to take Edward aside and explain.

He dressed quietly, reserving his flamboyance – as at Oxford – for his surroundings. A celebrated Norman Parkinson photograph has him seated at an ornate desk: silken swags billow from above; behind him is a Picasso pastel, 'Femme assise au chapeau'. His lunch-party guests would include such socially acceptable eccentrics as the actress Iris Tree, the poet Edith Sitwell and the musician-nobleman Lord Berners, plus, say, Noël Coward. He took on a butler, Thomas Pope, who stayed with him twenty years. He had inherited a very good cellar from his mother.

The likenesses of him which survive from this period, including that of the back of his head, twice over, in a famous Magritte painting, give an idea of how he looked: elegant profile save for a rather small jaw; dark hair with a slight wave, expensively shaped to the head; and the smooth complexion that is so often remembered. He was small, but uniformly so, a slightly scaled-down man. Iris Tree's son Ivan Moffat, later a Hollywood writer, met him for the first time at one of Augustus John's parties down at Fordingbridge and carried away a particularly vivid image of Edward about to drive off at the wheel of a monstrous Mercedes tourer. It was Edward's foot that impressed him – 'a little foot on a powerful gas pedal'.

What he was able to accomplish in the creative field was a little venture into publishing. Resuming the interest in printing he had formed at Oxford, he came to an arrangement with the Curwen Press, renowned for its enterprising typography and its association with David Garnett. Edward told me that Garnett taught him about typefaces and so on, but this seems to have been one of the many crossed circuits that afflicted his reminiscences. The novelist had little to do with that aspect of publishing. The typographer was Oliver Simon. Anyway, under the imprint of 'The James Press', Curwen brought out Edward's first book of poems, *Twenty Sonnets to Mary*. Ascribed simply to 'Edward', the slender little volume is elegant in the extreme, with marbled boards, creamy paper, italic type. The poems, evidently written three years earlier are – well, just the sort of poems that any reasonably talented undergraduate of the period might have written during languid Oxford afternoons: stuffed with classical allusions and pastoral images.

> A jostling, swirling army of the air,
> has burst into these bosky, terraced glades,
> which earlier were tranquil as the shades
> of Proserpine's calm, whispering winter lair.

And so on and so on, fluent, facile and innocent of any real passion.

The second publication of the James Press, in 1931, was the one that made literary history. Edward switched to another printer, the Westminster Press, and to an author other than himself. He offered to publish a collection of verse by his Oxford chum John Betjeman, by now on the staff of the *Architectural Review*. They called it *Mount Zion: or In Touch with the Infinite*, the second part of the title added chiefly in order to support an illustration Edward had found in an old catalogue and wished to use on the cover. It showed a stout lady beatifically using an early telephone. Edward's later involvement suffered from formidable distractions that year – getting married, and two journeys to America. In his absence Betjeman was lavish with complimentary and review copies; the attention he won with this, his first book, was the foundation of his subsequent career. Thirty years on he closed the jingling account of his early life, *Summoned by Bells* with the publication of *Mount Zion* and grateful stanzas to its begetter.

Opus three from the press, also dated 1931, is *Laengselia*, cautiously described as a play by Faustulus, in fact a whimsical version of Hans Andersen's 'The Little Mermaid'. It contains some mild satire on the social scene: a mermaid bright young thing says 'how stupendously delighted', another undersea character is dismissed as a social climber who 'would struggle to the surface of any sea *any* day if she thought it was going to promote her socially'. Requiring a full orchestra, a mezzo-soprano and a *corps de ballet* able to swim about the stage with graceful flicks of their tails, it was understandably never produced. Its sole interest lies in its provenance. Edward wrote it for the woman he married that year, and who cured him of his more ethereal notions of love.

6

Edward had first set eyes on Tilly Losch in the Noël Coward revue *This Year of Grace*, which C. B. Cochran put on in 1928. There were two star dancers in it: Jessie Matthews, as English as can be, and Tilly, who was half Slavonic, half Jewish and wholly Viennese. Edward was bowled over, particularly by her performance of a number called 'Gothic' in which she took up all the positions associated with thirteenth and fourteenth century sculpture, though perhaps not everyone in the audience would have appreciated this nicety. The music was Bach's 'Air on a G String'. 'Because I associated her with such beautiful music and beautiful sculpture,' Edward would confide, 'I thought she must have a beautiful soul.' Well, he was only twenty-one. He walked all round London trying to engineer an introduction, finally succeeding through an interior decorator who was doing some work for Tilly's mother.

Almost his first question to her was, 'Did you devise the choreography yourself, Miss Losch?' She said, 'Yes, I did,' though Edward later discovered it was the work of her former partner

35

Harald Krenzberg. Thus securely based on art rather than life, the courtship meandered on for the next two years. Once Edward climbed into her house in Curzon Street and she made it clear he could stay, but he was too shy, too naïve, he said in retrospect, too full of romantic ideals. He went off to Rome, though returning to London for one week especially to see her.

Of all the portraits of Tilly that survive, the one that most captures her disturbing sexuality is that made a few years on by Pavel Tchelitchew for the *Ballets 1933* programme. The huge, moody eyes gaze out from between high cheekbones – she had no trouble playing a Chinese in the film of *The Good Earth* later still. The mouth is full, the chin like a little girl's – according to Edward, she would accent it lightly with rouge if she wanted to give herself a little-girl look. One elfin ear peeps out from thick hair hanging straight. She was not very tall, certainly not willowy, but amazingly graceful in her movements. Her eyes were glass-blue-green. She had a bloom to her, says Diana Gould (Lady Menuhin), who as a very young dancer worked with her twice; men were drawn to her; she was a born *allumeuse*, a pleasing French expression meaning, literally, one who lights men up.

She was born in November 1904, making her nearly three years older than Edward, studied at the Court ballet school and joined the Vienna State Opera ballet in 1921. She was a soloist by 1924, as well as playing straight roles at the Burgtheater. Max Reinhardt cast her in his

Midsummer Night's Dream at Salzburg in 1927, for which she also did the choreography. C. B. Cochran, ever on the look-out for popular stars among exponents of the higher arts, completed her transition to revue and musical comedy. She was very graceful, very feminine, very temperamental. She shared a dressing room with Jessie Matthews and they squabbled frequently as to whether the window should, or should not, be open. She was in another West End show, *Wake Up and Dream*, in 1929, then went to America.

Edward went to see her in New York early in 1931, and in the language of the light fiction of the day, popped the question. They were married within a week, on 4 February, at a church on Fifth Avenue. Edward lent the bride his car and went by taxi with his best man, Prince von Fürstenberg – unfortunately, to the wrong church. Tilly, kept waiting, wasn't amused. She wore a rather everyday outfit of clipped lamb coat and matching hat, which Edward decided, in retrospect, was chosen to indicate that no undue importance should be attached to the occasion. The guests nevertheless included Edward's immensely rich uncle (or, strictly, his cousin) Arthur Curtis James and his wife Harriet. The happy couple left first for Chicago, where Edward's sister Audrey – now married to the newspaper publisher Marshall Field – gave them dinner before they boarded the train for San Francisco.

In the night Edward surprised Tilly by his ardour. 'You're rather a good lover,' she murmured, gratified. 'That makes something a little extra.' From his boyish looks and boyish manner, and – it should be conceded – his reticence before marriage, she had been quite convinced that, like so many young men around the theatre, he was queer. She remained half-convinced of it, or alternatively chose to revive the suspicion as soon as she tired of the marriage – she professed the belief that 'modern marriages need last only a few months', and when on the second day the train stopped at Reno, said, not absolutely in jest, 'Let's have the divorce now.'

Even the honeymoon in Hawaii (Edward had really intended it to be Tahiti but confused the two names) was the occasion for subsequent recriminations. There was this beach-boy Edward kept photographing and whom Tilly once found with him in their room. Edward, it must be said, had an extraordinary knack of recounting these stories to put himself in the worst possible light, protesting just a shade too vehemently, elaborating just a degree more than was necessary. Yes, he did take a lot of photographs of the boy, because he was such a beautiful human being, but the only time he came into their room was on the day they were leaving, to help Edward close his trunk . . .

Who wouldn't jump to the obvious conclusions? Yet he really did seem to be desperately in love with Tilly, and the honeymoon must also have had its sweetnesses. There is a photograph of them together on the beach, rather touching in its ordinariness. Tilly is wearing owlish spectacles – she was short-sighted – and Edward is wrapped in a towelling bath-robe. He wrote a poem 'To Ottilie'

(Ottilie Ethel Losch being her full name), likening their relationship to a mirage seen in the desert, or a sea with distant sail upon it, which is a miracle of heartfelt simplicity by the side of the *Mary* sonnets:

> I your lover, you my wife
> Until we dissolve and are
> Just as that mirage seen from far,
> A sudden sparkle on a sea
> Which is, yet only seems to be.

On the way back they stopped off in Palm Springs to see a friend and fellow Austrian of Tilly's, Count Friedrich Ledebur. He was a giant of a man, married to Iris Tree and later a film actor, most famously as Queequeg in John Huston's *Moby Dick*. Tilly told Edward, 'You must meet him. He's so big and jolly,' and curiously the two men did get on very well together despite a difference in height of over a foot; but only a few months later Edward found that Tilly had been citing Ledebur as representative of the raffish Bohemain set into whose company her husband had drifted.

Edward had planned to take Tilly back to England for the summer. The staff at Wimpole Street and also at West Dean, at last available to him, had been instructed to have everything ready. But without his knowing, he claimed, she had signed up for the musical *The Band Wagon* with Adele and Fred Astaire. Edward went to the opening in Philadelphia. Helen Broderick, a tough old Broadway actress in the cast, took one look at him and said to Tilly, 'Does your husband travel half-fare?' Edward always claimed to have been amused by this, only Tilly was furious. Had Broderick happened to hit on one of the less obvious strains in the match – a beautiful woman already aware the bloom must fade, and married a someone not only her junior in years but looking absurdly younger still? Or was it simply the impossibility of two such ill-sorted people ever accommodating to each other?

Tilly had been a working girl from childhood; Edward's dilettantism must have been as baffling to her as it was infuriating. She was also a model of the ambitious performer for whom career always came first. Children had no part in her plans, while Edward yearned for an heir. Here, in the early days of the marriage, he believed, she engineered the first of the four abortions he eventually accused her of having had. Three were alleged to have happened during the American sojourn. An abortion in those days was medically much more arduous. How Tilly was supposed to have fitted three of them into an unbroken theatre run was not made clear. Which is not to doubt the pain Edward felt when once the question of abortion was being discussed and he said, 'Wouldn't it prevent you having children in the future?' and she snapped back – he would imitate the coldness in her voice – 'Don't be silly!'

Edward, for his part, could hardly have been worse prepared by upbringing for the give and take of marriage. His father had died when he was five, his mother-figure had been chased away. His youngest sister was seven years his senior. He was spoiled and yet deprived, generous yet wary, full of romantic notions about the fusion of souls but blind to the practical need to adjust attitudes. In his many stories of life with Tilly, recalled in painful detail, he never said 'us' or 'we' or 'our'. It was always my house, my child, my friends, Tilly's friends.

The Band Wagon settled into a run at the New Amsterdam Theatre on West 42nd Street. They lived in a rented house on Park Avenue. For something to do, Edward learned to fly a plane, and first visited the Mexican border that would so attract him in later years. In the autumn he learned from someone, somehow, that the National Government which had succeeded Labour was planning to take Britain off the Gold Standard. He sailed on the *Bremen*, spent three hectic days in London attempting to sell stock that would be affected and caught the same liner back after its turn-around in Germany. During one or other of these absences Tilly entertained an admirer, Prince Serge Obolensky.

7

Finally, Edward was able to take his wife home to England. But where was home? Wimpole Street was being refurbished to flatter Tilly, with the Paul Nash bathroom in alabaster and a white-on-white bedroom designed by Edward himself. In the meantime they moved into a mews house at 3 Culross Street, off Grosvenor Square, which Edward had acquired, or had been persuaded to acquire by his sister Audrey, against just such an eventuality. Before she married Marshall Field, Audrey made a business of buying unpromising flats and houses, doing them up and selling them.

While they were in America, Edward had lent this house to Randolph Churchill, who had kept his latch-key and would sometimes drop in on them in the middle of the night. Perhaps for this reason, perhaps because a proper W1 address appealed to Tilly's sense of values, she was always happiest there. Then there was West Dean.

The house had been let since 1917 to a family called Sturdy. This was the famous long let at a peppercorn rent which so aggrieved Edward as he grew up. His sister Millicent's husband Henry

Howard (of the Mowbray Howards, the Duke of Norfolk's family), who succeeded Uncle Arthur as trustee, had engineered it, Edward forever maintained, solely in pursuance of his prolonged affair with Mrs Sturdy. Mr Sturdy was so pleased to have a stately home and all its garden produce for next to nothing that he turned a blind eye to their goings-on. The baffling element in this story is how the Sturdys managed to afford living at West Dean, peppercorn rent or no. When Edward finally moved into his rightful home, even he – a millionaire – found it too big and costly.

If Tilly had taken to the place, perhaps things would have been different. Edward certainly directed some of his most extravagant attempts at pleasing her to this end. To make it easier for her to travel down there after the theatre, he ordered from the coachbuilders a special Rolls-Royce, copied from one he'd seen of Lord Louis Mountbatten's, in which the seats folded down to make a bed. When, in stepping from her bath in the big house, Tilly left wet foot-marks on the floor, he commissioned a roll of Axminster stair-carpet immortalizing her footprint – a romantic gesture only slightly devalued by a similar carpet he ordered later which did the same for the muddy pawmarks of a favourite dog.*

* It also has to be admitted that the Tilly's footprint carpet, having been completed and delivered after the lady herself had gone, was not actually laid until 1948. In due course it became worn and in 1989 the Edward James Foundation imaginatively had a fresh length woven.

43

The trouble was that Tilly was a city girl who loved city life, theatres, crowds. And to jump ahead a few months, if nothing else had put her off West Dean, the traumatic night when she suffered – or started to suffer – a miscarriage would surely have done so. Meanwhile it was Edward who mostly used the special Rolls, driven down to West Dean in the small hours by his faithful chauffeur and left there, parked under the porch, snoozing away in clean pyjamas between clean sheets, until his equally faithful butler woke him at 10 a.m. with orange juice and coffee.

Most of all, he hankered to please his wife by furnishing her with a triumph in the theatre. His 'Little Mermaid' script could perhaps become more of an operetta, even a ballet. He commissioned a score from Georges Auric, but Auric never delivered it. Instead, Tilly went into a revival of *The Miracle*, the perfervid religious spectacle C.B. Cochran had put on at Olympia before the First World War. The story came from medieval legend and concerned a nun who leaves her devotions to go into the forest with her lover. A statue of the Madonna comes to life, takes her place and bears her punishment for her. The dramatization, in mime and music, was chiefly an opportunity for the great master of stage *schmalz*, Max Reinhardt, to achieve his effects.

He had aready revived the show with great success in New York and other American cities in 1924, when the English society beauty, Lady Diana Cooper, whose previous acting experience was limited to two silent films, played both the

Madonna and the nun, though not on the same night, as part of a curious *ménage a trois* of stars who, not without tears, shared the two leads between them. A further American tour, with Lady Diana as sole Madonna and Iris Tree as the nun, followed in 1926–7.

Now, in partnership with C.B. Cochran again, Reinhardt brought the spectacle back to London. The venue this time was the Lyceum Theatre, off the Strand, which in the Second World War became a dance hall. Its auditorium was being 'Losched up', as Edward put it, by the addition of plywood Gothic arches over the boxes to persuade the audience that they were in a cathedral. This curious coinage of his was not, I think, directed at Tilly, whose talent he always recognized, whatever else he found to say against her, but at the close little theatrical professoriate of Austrians and Germans who surrounded Tilly at this time and in his imagination conspired to turn her against him. There was Reinhardt himself, his various lieutenants who were all addressed as 'Doktor', and the supreme enemy, Dr Rudolf Kommer von Cernowitz, known as *kätzchen* or 'little cat', who among other things was Tilly's agent. Edward was once invited to a fancy-dress party whose host stipulated that each guest should go as the person he most hated in the world. Edward went as Dr Kommer.

Lady Diana was once more to be the Madonna; *The Miracle* was all she ever did in the theatre. Tilly was the nun, and it is possible that as a professional since girlhood she did not relish playing second fiddle to such an occasional star, especially when the latter's mother, the Duchess of Rutland, would haunt rehearsals hooting to Reinhardt, 'Not enough light on my daughter; too much on Miss Losch.' A high moment in the show came when the nun discarded her veil and escaped into the forest with her knight, whereupon the Madonna came to life in nine graceful movements, gathered up the veil with one more and let it float into place over her head. At rehearsals it always went beautifully. On the first night Edward was surprised to see Tilly tie a knot in the veil before she let it flutter to the ground. The Madonna, foxed, had to add a couple of less graceful movements before she could don it. At the celebration afterwards a chill silence greeted Tilly, but such was her magic, when she chose to turn it on, that by the end of the party she had charmed everyone, except perhaps Lady Diana, into forgiveness. Later in the run, the Madonna summoned Edward to her dressing room, bared her shoulder to reveal a cluster of flea-bites and said, 'Look what your darling wife has done now,' but Edward generously believed that they were none of Tilly's doing, it was just an old theatre.

The revival failed to repeat the success of the earlier productions, though Lady Diana toured it round the provinces the following autumn. Among the chorus of nuns, all dancers, was the sixteen-year-old 'Cochran Understudy of the Year', Diana Gould. Offered the choice of understudying either Tilly or her namesake, she had plumped for the latter and later regretted it, for Lady Diana remained obstinately healthy while poor Tilly did in the end miss a few performances. She must already have been expecting when the show was in rehearsal. During the run, of course, her pregnancy became evident – ominously so to Diana Gould. 'The things one had to do in *The Miracle* would have given anyone a miscarriage,' she says.

In fact this sad event occurred several weeks after the end of the Lyceum season. In between there had been an acrimonious holiday in Venice and at least one social occasion back in London – the opening of Ciro's, the night club – when Tilly had notoriously danced all night. Edward was soon accusing her of having done so deliberately, together with wearing tight corsets and smoking too many cigarettes. Alternatively he would say she had taken quinine to bring on the abortion. Tilly counter-claimed that Edward was trying to poison her. Her supporters insist that she was heartbroken at losing her child.

What all accounts agree on is that the dramatic haemorrhage which signalled the wretched mishap occurred during a house party at West Dean which Edward held in September or October. The purpose was to introduce Tilly to the estate staff and incidentally demonstrate to her that life in the country could be glamorous. The guests included John Sutro, Cecil Beaton, Oliver Messel and Syrie Maugham and her daughter Liza. Among the less famous were Diana Gould and yet another Diana, Edward's niece Diana Beresford (née Howard), with her sister Pamela. They were still young girls, nineteen and seventeen, and remember being packed off to bed when Oliver Messel started telling rather risqué stories in the little ground-floor salon that had been Mrs Willie's boudoir. Later they were both wakened by people bursting unceremoniously into their rooms to take the quilts from their beds. 'John Sutro took mine,' says Diana. 'And Syrie Maugham mine,' says Pamela. They were wanted for Tilly, who had been taken ill. In Edward's version of events the baby wasn't finally lost until some days later, when the doctors told him that Tilly might be in danger if they didn't operate. The child would have been a boy.

The next volume from the James Press, which in fact was called *The Next Volume*, contained Edward's Hawaiian poems, with decorations by Rex Whistler. The book is dated 1932, but a correction slip reads, 'Publication of this book was withheld until January 1933 owing to the serious illness of the author's wife.'

8

Tilly had to spend some weeks recuperating at West Dean. Edward bought her paints and pastels and encouraged her to try her hand, a kindly gesture which gave Tilly an interest she took up seriously in later life. But as soon as she was up and about again she grew restless. She flitted back to New York, ostensibly to see about a part in a new musical, in reality – Edward claimed – to look up her lover Serge Obolensky, an emigré Russian prince who was married to Alice Astor, acted as public relations adviser to a number of hotel chains and had lately become a United States citizen. According to Edward, she was trying to persuade him to leave his wife and marry her as soon as they could both obtain divorces.

Edward went to Paris and then on the South of France, where he fell into a little affair which not only restored some confidence in himself but also introduced him into circles which were to have a profound effect on his future. She was a married woman older than himself: Marie-Laure, Vicom-tesse de Noailles. She and her husband Charles had a house at Hyères. Through them he got to know the Aldous Huxleys, along the coast at Sanary. He admired a portrait of Marie-Laure by a relatively unknown Spanish painter hanging in the de Noailles's house; this led to his interest in, and eventual patronage of, Salvador Dalí. More immediately, she interested him in the hopes and plans of a group of artists working in the ballet. With the death of Diaghilev the Russian Ballet that had astonished and delighted Europe throughout the 1920s had divided into two factions, one led by Léonide Massine, the other by Georges Balanchine and Boris Kochno. Balanchine had formed a small company of ten dancers, and was looking for financial support. Would Edward chip in, say £2,000, along with Coco Chanel and the Polignacs and the de Noailles and everyone?

Edward went along to a rehearsal and was excited. The company was working on a new ballet, *Mozartiana*, to music actually by Tchaikovsky from a Mozart theme, and with décor by Christian Bérard. Other ballets were commissioned from contemporary composers and designers, awaiting only the means to go ahead. Edward threw himself into the venture. It was something in which he could invest ideas and inspiration as well as more and more money. Above all, by attaching to the investment the trifling condition that Tilly be invited to join the company, he secured the perfect opportunity of giving her the triumph she craved. Or such has been the accepted belief. In the words of Patrick Boyle (now the Earl of Glasgow), who made a television documentary about Edward in 1978, he embarked upon 'one of the most grandiose bids a rich man ever made to recapture the wife he loved'. A similar line was taken in the catalogue to the exhibition held in Brighton ten years later commemorating the ballets, to the exasperation of Tilly's biographer Ann-Marie Koller, who leads a school of thought highly sceptical of this romantic story. 'What a line of baloney!' is how she put it in a letter to me. Edward, she maintains, was far more interested in the opportunity he saw of setting himself up as a brilliant new impresario.

Whatever his motives, Edward furnished the largesse for *Les Ballets 1933* to expand in aim from a single programme of ballets to a repertory of five or six works, out of which any three might be performed on a given evening. The name of M. Edward James figured prominently in the brochure that was being designed. He also contributed a preface in sonorous French proclaiming that, as the title suggested, the ballets were very much of the moment; they represented no new theory or school of dance; they were the fruits of instinctive necessity. Instinctive necessity had included, in Edward's case, the necessity to accommodate Tilly in a company which already included an assured prima ballerina, Tamara Toumanova.

Toumanova would dance *Mozartiana*, also *Les Songes* to music by Darius Milhaud and designs by André Derain, and *Fastes*, same designer, music by Henri Sauguet. Assuming that Tilly would not be as technically proficient, Balanchine and Kochno suggested that she should be given a ballet which did not require any sustained points work. Edward proposed they should approach Pavel Tchelitchew, the Russian painter and scene designer he had known and admired since Edith Sitwell introduced them in London in 1929. The resulting ballet, which in fact was Tchelitchew's entire concept, was *L'Errante*, to Schubert's 'Wanderer' sonata as orchestrated by Koecklin; the dancer, searching for love and companionship through dream-like encounters, was required mainly to run around ahead of an enormous flowing green train. Edith Sitwell came to a performance and declared that she could see in the swirling garment the green of forests, the green of water.

Tilly had meanwhile demonstrated, in no uncertain fashion, that she was as classically competent as anyone. *Les Valses de Beethoven* was added, which used some Beethoven tunes orchestrated by Nicholas Nabokov (cousin of the writer Vladimir Nabokov) for a perfectly classical ballet of Apollo and Daphne. It was the sixth ballet and third vehicle for Tilly that owed most to Edward's own inspiration, proved to be the most controversial item of the season and is certainly the most enduring work to emerge from it. Edward's idea was to represent the divided nature of woman by having two dancers, one embodying the grasping, practical side, the other the romantic, passionate side. How much it derived from marriage with Tilly is anyone's guess. He wrote out a scenario and asked Kurt Weill, composer of *The Threepenny Opera* and *Mahagonny*, if he would write the music. Weill was interested but proposed using a singer instead of one dancer, with his usual collaborator Bertolt Brecht furnishing the poems ('lyrics' was hardly a word you used with Brecht) and their favourite interpreter Lotte Lenya – who was also Weill's wife – coming in to sing them. And they would get the designer who had done *Dreigroschenoper* in Germany, Caspar Neher.

Brecht was summoned from Berlin. Edward always maintained that he thus saved the playwright from the arrest of known communists which followed the Nazi's accession to power in January 1933. In fact Brecht had long planned his escape, and made it immediately after the Reichstag fire. At first he refused the commission on the grounds that he was unwilling to work for a Wall Street capitalist who fancied he could dabble in the arts, but, swayed by Weill, relented. The 'ballet with songs' was written in April and May. For a while the whole circus moved over to London and Edward put up composers, designers, hangers-on.

Les Ballets 1933 played first at the Théâtre des Champs-Élysées for three months. For the London run to follow there had to be two English soloists and two English members of the *corps de ballet*. One of the latter was the same Diana Gould who had been in *The Miracle*. 'One fateful day,' she recalls dramatically, 'we were told to go to Paris to start working with the company. At Calais the authorities demanded to see our *permis de travail*, and of course Edward had completely forgotten we would need them.' They had to wait all day before permission eventually arrived for them to complete their journey. But Lady Menuhin, as she is now, gives a vivid picture of Edward immersed in the enterprise.

'He would dart up and down the stalls to see the stage from different angles. Or if he was sitting in his seat he'd jump up and clap his hands in enthusiasm. He was in love with it all! He was a child, really – innocent, everyone's prey. Those Russians were just running away with his money. They had no interest in the box office. It would never occur to them to repeat a programme that had gone down very well. Oh, no! They had to try something new every time. We all hated the Brecht number, I remember, because of the awful costumes we had to wear – cloaks with holes for the eyes.'

And Tilly?

'Well, Balanchine didn't like her. He liked long, sinuous shapes and she was rather small and square. She owed her place to Edward's sponsorship of the ballets. I don't say that was the sole reason he did it. There is no doubt he fancied himself as another Diaghilev. But of course she came into the calculation. Unfortunately, they were already not talking, Tilly and Edward. I was one of the go-betweens, with Daniels the chauffeur, forever relaying messages between them.'

The Savoy Theatre housed the London season towards the end of the year. Although purists were disconcerted by its mixture of song, dance and speech – and especially the idea that a dancer (Tilly) should speak – the greatest acclaim was for the item Diana Gould so disliked, the 'Spectacle sur des pòemes de Bert Brecht'. It was called *Anna, Anna* (reflecting the duality of the heroine), but is better known today by the title by which it survives in the concert hall as well as the theatre, *The Seven Deadly Sins*.

L'Errante was also well received, despite its fair share of mishaps. Tchelitchew's décor, it was discovered at the last minute, couldn't be fire-proofed to meet the Lord Chamberlain's very strict regulations in London. The artist had to design and execute a new set in nine hours. Then, during one of the performances, another dancer trod on Tilly's fifteen-foot train and tore it. Tilly signalled to the *corps de ballet* to improvise, shot off stage and up the spiral staircase to her dressing room and was back in her rehearsal costume within three minutes. *L'Errante* was subsequently performed in America, and revived again after the war, by Lincoln Kirstein, to whom Edward assigned such rights as he had in the ballets – a matter not always very clear: Bert Brecht turned up on the stage in Copenhagen once to stop a performance of *Anna, Anna.*

Whether the season could be regarded as a popular success is a matter of disagreement. According to a letter from Tchelitchew to friends in Paris the London run, at least, was a fiasco. They could not fill even a small theatre compared with the theatres Diaghilev had filled. According to Edward it was full houses every night. But in compliance with the eternal law (or lore) of James, there was certainly no profit in the venture for the man who put up all the money. His role, as usual, was to pay out. The takings vanished into the costs of renting the theatres, transporting the scenery, engaging a full symphony orchestra and rewarding the cluster of talents he had drawn into the show. It cost him nearly £100,000. And if it had been intended to save his marriage, it failed.

9

The divorce was ugly. Another couple, if unable to avoid it altogether, would at least have arranged for a discreet parting of the ways. With Tilly and Edward, unfortunately, it was a case of irresistible bloody-mindedness up against immovable obstinacy. The final collision was precipitated, rather symbolically, by the party Edward planned for the *Les Ballets* company at the end of the London run. Tilly was living at Culross Street under an agreement giving her tenure of the little house as long as she refrained from further demands. Edward wanted the piano back for his party at Wimpole Street, and high-handedly sent removal men to fetch it. Tilly sued for its return. Edward said that she had thus broken the conditions of her occupancy. She demanded a divorce. Edward refused to consider the customary sporting routine whereby the husband, whether the guilty party or not, spent a solemnly observed night in Brighton with a professional co-respondent, leading in due course to an undefended – and therefore largely unreported – suit. He insisted on bringing his own action, alleging Tilly's adultery with Serge

Obolensky. Tilly retaliated by choosing to defend the case, which meant that the dirt was all reportable, and duly reported.

All sorts of luminaries found themselves in the witness box, from Sir Thomas Beecham to Randolph Churchill and Tom Mitford, both of whom, as it happened, had also been Tilly's lovers. The night-watchman of the house Edward had rented on Park Avenue was summoned from New York to testify to visits by Obolensky when Edward was away; more damningly, Edward's secretary of the time, Donald Neville-Willing,* spoke of seeing the prince naked in Tilly's bedroom. Tilly countered by accusing Edward of cruelty, together with implications of his homosexuality. She had Sir Patrick Hastings as Counsel. Edward had the younger, then less eminent Norman Birkett (latter Lord Birkett), who had no great difficulty in puncturing Tilly's more lurid romances. Edward was granted his decree but none of his friends would speak to him.

The memoirs of his early life that Edward delivered to a tape recorder for *Swans Reflecting Elephants*, it has to be said, are nowhere more gratingly self-justificatory than in the chapter devoted to the divorce. Tilly had evidently tried to exploit an episode in which Edward took up a

*An Englishman resident in New York in the 1930s. Later he became a successful hotel manager and, after the war, as Major Neville-Willing, manager of the Café de Paris in London. He wrote a nice description of Edward when young as looking 'like a bird, a little pedantic bird about to take off'.

strapping young Italian bus-driver he heard singing, and offered to pay for singing lessons for him. Once again – as with the Hawaiian beach-boy – he protests his disinterested motives just too vehemently. He goes on to brag of his skill and daring in the witness box, though from the examples he gives it is quite obvious he was airing a pertness that, if Tilly's evidence had been stronger, would have cost him dearly.

The rancour with which Edward evermore recalled the marriage, the light he put upon almost every one of Tilly's actions, the accusations he continued to level, were no prettier: she had only married him for his money, anticipating a straightforward annulment and handsome settlement as soon as she could discover, to her shock and dismay, that he was a homosexual; when this assumption turned out to be at least partly unfounded she set out to contrive it; *en route* she seduced his best friends; she refused to bear his children or as good as murdered the one she did carry. Then suddenly the resentment would be directed at friends and hangers-on who stayed under his roof and ate his food and drank his wine while Tilly was in hospital but sent her not even a bunch of violets; and just as nuclear physicists track invisible particles by their impact on other matter, you glimpsed for a moment the hollow left by the loss of her.

After another Cochran revue, *Streamline*, Tilly went to Hollywood to appear in *The Garden of Allah* and then *The Good Earth*, in which she played the adulteress. In 1939 she married the uxorious Earl of Carnarvon, but stayed with him only ten weeks before sailing once again to America. This marriage was dissolved in 1947; at the earl's insistence Tilly continued to style herself 'Countess of Carnarvon'. Her last film role of note was as the Mexican woman, Mrs Chavez, in the torrid Western *Duel in the Sun*. Later she introduced a television show sponsored by General Motors. She returned to London, settled in Eaton Square, began but did not complete an autobiography, and resumed the pastime which Edward had devised for her when she was convalescing after the miscarriage. She even held a couple of exhibitions. 'A pleasant Sunday painter,' said *The Times*. She died in 1975.

Serge Obolensky, a man of great charm and dash who had fought in the Tsarist Russian army in the First World War, enlisted in the American army in the Second and although nearly fifty became a parachutist, once dropping in on Sachie and Georgia Sitwell in Northamptonshire. As for Edward . . . In a poem written ten or twelve years later as part of a sequence called *For the Lonely*, he was still trying to exorcize a ghost.

> *I do at moments think about her yet –*
> explain to me how one so like a child
> could be so cruel, should be so false, so wild.
> Believe me this: – she spun a kind of net
> like some weird, magic spider with her charm
> about more men than me.
>
> > She still may harm
> My peace, unless you teach me to forget.

Yes, she was young; but, as one in a tower
surveys the world, detached. She loved a storm
and leaned towards the lightning to perform
dark rites; but pouted like a child when sour.
You want to pierce the nature of her power,
her face, her character, her tone, her form.
Now, understand, she was not kind, nor warm;
and you do for me daily in one hour
more loving, gentle things than she in all
the months she knew me ever did. The sum
of every sweetness she accorded then
would never total half which I recall
you gave me yesterday.
                                      My darling, come
let us not ever mention her again.

Ironically, in the light of Tilly's accusations, the
next sonnet in the sequence makes it clear that the
new loved one is a man.

10

Exhausted, ostracized and drained of emotion, Edward withdrew to West Dean and sought to busy himself with the concerns of a country landowner. When, in November 1934, the little church nestling against the walls of the big house was almost destroyed by fire, he threw himself into its restoration. Why not rebuild it in a style to accord with the house as modified by Wyatt? He went to the Soane Museum and found among the designs of Sir John Soane one for a City church, anticipating the Gothic Revival, which in fact had never been built. John Betjeman, one of the few friends who had stayed loyal to him, knew an architect who was willing to adapt the plans to what remained of the old church. Alas, the churchwardens turned down the scheme. Edward's ballet season was still fresh in memory and, said the local virago, 'We don't want any of Mr James's Russian ballet nonsense down here in Sussex.' Edward nevertheless contributed handsomely towards the rebuilding costs – as he did when the tower required further restoration half a century later – and is named on a commemorative plaque in the church.

He acquired an Irish wolfhound, and walked the miles of his estate. The arboretum that Willie James had planted with exotics brought back from his travels was a favourite destination. Edward added to it; he loved trees, he loved growing things. He even worked up a zeal for competitive horticulture. There was a new gardener, the Chelsea Flower Show was in the offing again. They prepared an entry of fine arum lilies; Edward was bitterly disappointed when he failed to win first prize, blaming the new gardener's poor staging of their display. And one evening in the early summer of that year, 1935, he experienced an extraordinary vision or hallucination, whichever way you account for these things. He was eating his solitary dinner. Suddenly the dining-room ceiling seemed to part, and to the music of Beethoven's *Eroica* he saw a great swirling vision of the creation of the world. He was so overcome he had to leave the table and go into another room, where presently his puzzled butler found him.

The whole phenomenon lasted some ten or fifteen minutes. Edward has no doubt it was subjective, but bursting to record the experience he found himself casting it in the form of a novel, ascribing it to someone for whom it was utterly real. *The Gardener Who Saw God* is almost the only book of Edward's to enjoy normal commercial publication (by Duckworth). Indeed it ran into a second edition, and an American edition. It is also by far his best prose work, one of those lone novels (like Eugène Fromentin's *Dominique*) with a sharp individuality which the author never attempts again. It is so very nearly very good that its digressions and irrelevancies and knowing asides and little bits of moralizing are all the more irritating.

The story opens with the incident that Edward resourcefully took from recent first-hand experience – driving up to the Chelsea Flower Show with a collection of orchids and lilies, being unable to display them to full advantage because the proper staging hasn't arrived, and having to be content with second prize instead of first. The detail is so vivid that the reader is drawn into the hopes and fears of the hero, supposedly a humble gardener called Joseph Smith, despite a gathering certainty that the author knows very little about humble persons of any calling.

Joseph is gentle, conscientious, uncommunicative. He has been subjected to the same injustice which Edward encountered, only scaled down to hundreds of pounds rather than tens of thousands, of being obliged to settle his late mother's debts while four elder siblings pocket their share of the estate. He has suffered from the rejections of a calculating Irish girl who has some of the attributes of Tilly. He has also been married to an idealized girl who died young, which may represent the philosophy made fashionable in the plays of Jean Anouilh a few years later, that death is the only true way of keeping love alive. He is endowed by the author with an instinctive appreciation of art and music.

There are also plenty of above-the-stairs

characters drawn sardonically from the world more familiar to Edward. Mrs Deathon Astring was based on Lady Colefax, the interior designer, Lady Judas Iscariot on Lady Juliet Duff, Lady Marionette on Nancy Cunard – but there are references to Lady Cunard under her own name as well, as a bit of clever double-bluff. An eccentric Lord Bullborough, who has giant ears built on to his house and a grand piano in a tree, is clearly inspired by the real-life eccentric and friend of Edward's, Gerald Berners, who built a famous folly on his estate at Faringdon and dyed his tame pigeons pretty colours.

There is a tiresome surrealist poet who is given a whole chapter in which to expound the surrealist creed to a bemused Joseph, and a pretty girl in the swimming pool who turns out, perhaps significantly perhaps not, to have been born the same year as Edward James and have the same rather clouded paternity. It is altogether such a ragbag of different stuffs that it shouldn't have any cohesion, yet in some strange way it does. Towards the end the narrative returns to the starting point, and Joseph's mood at the end of the long day following the flower show disappointment. He has travelled back to the big house with the one really splendid character in the story, the old housekeeper Mrs Magginery. For some reason Edward had modelled the house not on West Dean but on Castle Howard in Yorkshire. Mrs Magginery, however, was quite obviously Mrs McKay, the West Dean housekeeper. What follows is related in a sustained, strange, haunting hundred or more pages. The family is away. Drawn to the library Joseph studies the absent master's books and pictures, plays his records on his gramophone. A carved figure brought back from Spain crashes mysteriously to the floor. Upstairs in her room old Mrs Magginery suffers a heart attack and, all alone, grumbling to herself, dies. The clock ticks away the hours. Joseph at last goes back to his cottage, drinks some red wine (he is a gardener of eclectic tastes), and wanders out again into the hushed night garden.

> Then in the lower part of the sky, towards the horizon to the left of the elms, very imminent he saw taking colour as well as form and gaining in precision, flocks and flocks of those small white spring gladioli with butterfly markings that are named Nymph gladioli . . . rapidly, kaleidoscopically, as if by a big wind the formation of the cloud-built flowers became puffed into larger and larger contours. And now they were no longer clouds at all, but real petals of moist and breathing flowers filling the entire heaven. . .

The vision proceeds in a great set piece, from botanic to zoological to apocalyptic images, all swirling and whirling in the sky, until:

> Joseph dared no longer look up. Something was going to explode above . . . He did not see the sudden flash or hear the roar that came: he felt them: he received a heavy physical

blow upon his head and shoulders and fell for a moment senseless to the ground.

When it was published two years later *The Gardener* attracted glowing reviews from Richard Church, Howard Spring, Harold Brighouse, Frank Swinnerton and *Country Life* ('There is a description of the Royal Horticultural Show which alone would make the book worth reading'), and one by James Agate from which the publishers could at least extract a favourable quote for the second-edition wrapper. The cover design of Joseph squinting up at the gathering vision out of the corner of his eye, as if not daring to turn full face to it, was by Tchelitchew.

11

Edward had loved pictures from his earliest years when, lying in bed at night or in the morning, he constructed fantasies around a picture of a medieval city that hung on his nursery wall. It became a private world, the 'little city of Seclusia' that figured many years later in his own painting and may even have inspired – why not? – his architectural fantasies in Mexico. It was certainly the inspiration for *Reading into the Picture*, the little fairy-tale epic he had published in 1934, between *The Next Volume* and *The Gardener*.

Child, would you enter this fantastic town
whose walls are yellow and whose roofs are
   brown.
A bridge, full-arched, can lead you to the gate
over a river which is still in spate

– as so often with Edward's verse, three good lines and then a flat-footed one, but the idea behind the poem is still a valuable one. If, as is claimed, the average time spent before a picture in our public galleries is a matter of seconds rather than minutes, any attempt to draw people into looking a little deeper is to be encouraged.

Though he was always buying curios and couldn't pass a demolition site without nosing in and making an offer for the Regency mouldings or rococo down-pipes, Edward had not so far – rather surprisingly – emerged as a collector of pictures. The one *coup* of which he was proud dated from the 1929 visit to Berlin to see the Nicolsons and Christopher Sykes. In a commercial gallery on the Unter den Linden he spotted a scene of birds against a landscape of forest and hills receding into the distance, full of the mysterious, enchanted quality that appealed to him. It was a Jan Breughel, the twin of a better-known version in the Palazzo Doria in Rome. Thanks to the runaway inflation of the German mark, Edward was able to buy it, together with an attestation from the director of the gallery, for a mere £300.

It was because he couldn't find any more old masters at such prices, he used to profess, that he started to patronize young contemporary artists. He began with those from whom he had commissioned designs, whether for books or ballets or whatever. The prodigiously gifted draughtsman Rex Whistler was probably the first. Whistler could – and did, when he joined the army in 1940 – make a work of art of a diagram of how a guardsman was to lay out his kit for inspection. His murals still adorn the Tate Gallery's restaurant. For Edward, apart from illustrating two or three books, he designed a Neptune carpet to go in the dining room at West Dean and the oak carvings, to be executed by the renowned Englishes, father and sons, in what became known as the Oak Room.

Then there was Jörg von Reppert-Bismarck, a descendant of the Iron Chancellor who, if not quite such a catch in the long run, furnished nice enough pictures for *Reading into the Picture*. But the deviser of Tilly's earthbound ballet and jacket illustrator of *The Gardener* was the first whose works he seems to have set out to collect, and continued to collect. Pavel Tchelitchew (sometimes spelt with a final *–ff*) was a Russian aristocrat who fled the aftermath of the Revolution, joined a travelling theatre in Turkey as scene-painter in exchange for bed and board, and eventually landed up in Paris among all the other starving artists.

He was discovered by Gertrude Stein. Through her he met Edith Sitwell. Edith adored him; unfortunately he was a homosexual of the thoroughness which only a Russian aristocrat could bring to such matters, but he was fond of her company. He painted her many times: one portrait, in which she is famously depicted as a sybil, still hangs in West Dean; another belongs to the Sitwell family. In this, her extraordinary profile ('like the back of a spoon', said Donald Neville-Willing, who had met everyone who was anyone) is set squarely against a rich, Renaissance-like background as in a Piero della Francesca likeness of a Florentine worthy. Yet from the same period Edward owned a Tchelitchew modishly assembled from sequins. Other works eventually in his

70

possession displayed the artist's remarkable draughtsmanship – a portrait head made up of fine concentric lines, like contours on a map; a hollow skull seen as a hologram; a human eye so detached and spherical and luminously blue that twenty or thirty years ahead of the Apollo programme it uncannily resembles one of those photographs of Earth seen from space.

Pavel was an exuberant, touchy character who would go from high spirits to sudden rages and back again. When Edith took him to stay with her brother Sacheverell at Weston Hall, he stormed out one morning because he had found in the guest room a book about painting which he decided had been deliberately left there to insult him. But he could also be good company. He arrived at West Dean during Edward's year of rustication, ostensibly to paint a fresco round the great staircase. In the event this never got done, but he did much to cheer up Edward, despite bringing along his tiresome new boy-friend, a willowy young southern American called Charles Henri Ford. Charles Henri was co-author of an apparently pornographic novel which Tchelitchew kept extolling, and a poet who believed in random juxtaposition, opening the dictionary at hazard, picking out a word, opening it again.

'Why don't you do the same, Edward?' Tchelitchew would tactlessly bray. 'You'll never get anywhere while you're so conservative.' Edward pretended to arrive at Keats's 'Ode to a Nightingale' by this method, but the painter refused to see either virtue in the poem or irony in the gesture.

Another story Edward frequently told was of the time he bought no less than eight of Pavel's paintings at an exhibition and Pavel, instead of showing humble gratitude, immediately embarked upon a harangue about his (Edward's) true talent in life being that of A Collector, on which he should henceforth concentrate all his energy, e.g. by buying yet more Tchelitchews. Charles Henri was supposed to have put his head close to the artist's and murmured, 'Pavel, je crois que tu fais des gaffes.'

Despite such misunderstandings and – worse – the occasional all too accurate understanding, together with the usual suspicions on Edward's part that he was being overcharged or taken for granted, the visit went on to last for some months. Soon afterwards, Tchelitchew returned to America with Charles Henri to settle there permanently. He had already (in December 1934) held a successful one-man show at the Julien Levy Galleries in New York. He decided now that America offered the best prospects for art, mankind and, not least, Pavel Tchelitchew. He embarked upon the giant canvas that is commonly supposed to be his master-piece, *Phenomena*, to be found in the Tretyakov State Gallery, Moscow. Obsessed since his travelling show days, perhaps, by human oddities, he filled a surrealist landscape with Siamese twins, bearded women and other freaks, many of whom bore striking resemblances to his friends and patrons. For Edward James there was a special role, as the model for one head of a two-headed man; the other head was the artist's own.

12

Though Tchelitchew liked to think he kept a foothold in the surrealist camp, and *Phenomena* was certainly bizarre enough to count as a surrealist work, he was always classed as a neo-romantic; that is, modern in his urge to experiment but traditional in his choice of subject and sometimes nostalgic in its treatment, as in that Florentine profile of Edith Sitwell. Others lumped in the category included Christian Bérard and the Berman brothers, Léonid and Eugène. Edward bought pictures by them all, but it was with the surrealists, a much more self-conscious and self-promoting group of artists, that his name became forever linked.

His involvement with them, and with art and artists of the period in general, can be charted in the pages of *Minotaure*, an avant-garde magazine of the arts with which he was characteristically associated. It was produced by the Paris publisher Albert Skira, who was also issuing a series of reproductions of French paintings. Edward put money into both projects and in the end, inevitably, fell out with Skira, but the earlier *Minotaures*, at all events, show his influence. The very first issue devoted two pages to a facsimile of Kurt Weill's *Anna, Anna* score, then newly composed. His favourite artists, Tchelitchew and Dalí, designed covers and title pages, as did Picasso. His own contributions included poems (in French) with drawings by Dalí and a mock-learned dissertation (also in French) on Queen Mary's formidable hats. Though publication was supposed to be quarterly, it was in practice sporadic; in all there were thirteen issues betwen 1933 and 1939, the last two bound together as a double number.

It wasn't all modernism. Edward also contributed a piece in English, 'The Marvel of Minuteness,' in praise of sixteenth-century portrait miniatures he had come across in Vienna. Someone else wrote about the Pre-Raphaelites. The camera reportage of Bill Brandt was represented. But the true predilection of the editorial policy was implicit in the interests declared on the mast-head: 'Arts Plastiques, Poésie, Musique, Architecture, Ethnologie, Mythologie, Spectacles, Psychologie, Psychiatrie, Psychanalyse' – give or take a couple of items, the hobby-horses of the surrealists.

Surrealism didn't just happen. It was formulated quite deliberately, out of the debris of several wild and woolly art movements, notably the nihilist Dada group whose more famous exploits had included a reproduction of the Mona Lisa decorated with a moustache and supplied with an obscene caption, and the Cologne exhibiton of 1920 at which visitors were invited to smash the exhibits with a chopper, helpfully provided. It also owed much to fashionable theories of psychology emanating from Freud. The *Manifesto of Surrealism*, published in 1924 by André Breton, founder and leader of the movement, decried the rationalism and logic which ruled the world and urged instead that fantasy, superstition and the unconscious mind be explored in the search for truth. Surrealism, in a famous if grim definition that followed, was 'Pure psychic AUTOMATISM, by which it is intended to express verbally, in writing or in any other way, the true process of thought. It is the dictation of thought, free from the exercise of reason and every aesthetic or moral preoccupation.'

In practice, automatism proved rather difficult to engineer, especially in painting. Writers could scribble down stream-of-consciousness prose or the kind of poem Tchelitchew recommended to Edward. Works of art could be 'found' by signing a bicycle wheel, filling a bird-cage with lumps of sugar or arranging a pile of bricks, a tradition which was to survive. But how could the act of putting paint on canvas be freed from conscious design? Max Ernst devised a technique of *frottage*, whereby he took rubbings of surfaces that appealed to him and transferred them to his canvas. André Masson flung glue at the canvas, then sand, and used the randomly textured surface as the starting point for his picture.

Most surrealist painters, however, and all the ones associated with Edward James, quickly abandoned experimental techniques, forgot about automatism and applied old-fashioned painterly skills to the pursuit of the Freudian ideal in surrealism. They sat in darkened rooms to try and induce that state between sleep and waking when dreams float up. They released secret erotic fantasies. They created grotesque creatures, mapped dream-like landscapes and showed people frozen in incongruous predicaments. Paul Delvaux's downy nudes waited patiently in empty stations or benighted streets. Paul Roy inserted into the most ordinary interior a snake slithering down the stairs. Joan Miró refined the dream world into shapes and colours.

Edward was always drawn to artists who were not yet well established, who were still relatively young. He pretended he couldn't afford better-known names, though he had a sheaf of Picasso etchings as well as the splendid gouache behind his desk in Wimpole Street. It seems much likelier that he enjoyed discovery for its own sake, and then backing his judgement with his cheque book. Of the surrealists, founding fathers such as Max Ernst or André Masson never figured in Edward's collection. While greatly admiring Miró, he did not collect him. He acquired only a single Delvaux – admittedly the highly desirable 'La Comédie du Soir', also known as 'Les Belles de Nuit'. His great favourites at this time were Dalí (to whom we will come in due course), René Magritte and Leonor Fini.

Fini was then in her late twenties, a beautiful Italian-Argentine living in Paris and painting elegant, often erotic fantasies. In cooler moods she was also a fine draughtsman. The most celebrated work of hers that Edward owned was known simply as 'Composition with Figures on a Terrace', two young men and three tousled girls – one of them usually assumed to be a self-portrait – looking rather spent; someone's discarded stocking is draped over a step in the terrace. It's a marvellous picture, though just what has been going on is anyone's guess.

Magritte, like Delvaux, was Belgian. Edward first admired him from a distance, then got to know him through Dalí. They became friends. 'What a nice man he was,' says Edward, in what must be almost his only unqualified testimonial to a fellow human being. Magritte came to stay at Wimpole Street and was charged with a commission that has now become legendary. Edward had four tall looking-glasses with lunettes by Boucher depicting the four seasons. They had come from his father's town house in Bryanston Square. After Magritte had finished with them they were set up on the handsome staircase at No. 35; visitors there remember vividly the moment when Edward would press a switch and what they had thought to be rather dark mirrors were suddenly lit from behind to reveal four new, and complementary, pictures by the Belgian. Magritte added to the surrealist vision a strong metaphysical quality. He took everyday reality and gave it a disconcerting inversion, as in the much-mentioned 'portrait' of Edward gazing into a mirror; you see the back of the subject's head, and reflected in the glass, the back of his head again. A similar picture slots Magritte's own features into a cut-out at the back of the head. In a third, Edward's face has become a blur of light.

One of the best-known Magrittes, 'Time Transfixed', is an almost photographic account of a fireplace in a sparsely furnished room. The marble surround, the wall panelling each side of it, the clock that stands on the marble top, its reflection – a proper reflection this time – in the overmantel mirror, the graining of the floor-boards, are all meticulously detailed. Through the blank partition sealing off the hearth projects a steam locomotive, its plume of smoke drawn up the chimney. The whole effect is so solid, so matter-of-fact, that when an Irish journal came across old photographs of a bizarre rail accident in Dublin, with just such a locomotive poking out over the street, it wondered if the incident might have been Magritte's inspiration, and reproduced his picture alongside the actuality. Someone sent Edward a copy; far from scoffing, he rather enjoyed the supposition.

The appeal that Magritte and Delvaux and the others had for Edward lay partly in this solidity, this professional competence. He loathed abstract painting and though an amateur himself could not stand amateurishness in others. To be a surrealist painter of the kind he admired you had first to be a superb realist. Beyond this, and beyond the accident that they happened to be up and coming (and, as he says, available) when he was engaged in the art world, the surrealists' imagery and the surrealists' philosophy attracted him strongly. Since infancy he had loved dreams, fantasies, magic worlds. As a rich man debarred from making a name for himself by the approved dogged struggle, he welcomed the rejection of the ordinary rules and the pursuit of chance. As somone who hated routine or committing himself ahead, he embraced the idea of dedicating his life to the unexpected.

13

All this time, of course, Edward had been steadily emerging from his seclusion. The complicated business of enjoying life had to be resumed. He flew an aeroplane down to Cap Ferrat to see Syrie Maugham and was arrested for landing on the beach without bothering about customs formalities. He sailed a yacht around the Greek islands. He motored in France and Spain, and rented from Lord Grimthorpe a villa in Italy, the Villa Cimbrone at Ravello, above Amalfi. Here he was so happy that he agreed to take it for the next seven years, though the tide of history was to cut short the arrangement. An early sign of the times was an empty place as Edward's guests gathered at Ravello in 1936: among those invited had been the poet Federico García Lorca, murdered in the first days of the Spanish Civil War.

That same year Edward was immersed in the first of two affairs of the heart which helped him to get over the divorce. She was the German-Norwegian dancer Brigitta Hartwig, who danced with the Monte Carlo ballet under the name of Vera Zorina and was herself recovering from an unhappy affair with Léonide Massine. She was beautiful in sunny Nordic style, the very opposite of Tilly, with a slim figure (as long as she watched her diet) and the film star legs so prized in the 1930s and 1940s. She went to a party at Wimpole Street and was much impressed by the huge bowl of lilies in the hall, perfuming the house. She also approved of the way Edward had invited his débutante nieces along with the celebrities. She was only nineteen herself.

Later in the summer Edward went to see her in Berlin, where she was staying with her widowed mother while awaiting the call to star in the London production of the Rodgers and Hart musical *On Your Toes*, which was choreographed by Georges Balanchine. Unfortunately this kept being postponed and Brigitta was having to tide herself over by performing at the Wintergarten, the city's big variety theatre. The Berlin Olympic Games, intended to convince the world of Nazi supremacy, were in full swing. Edward and the Hartwigs were given the best seats at the stadium because Mutti had been the mistress, on and off for fifteen years, of an interesting minor figure in the annals of the Third Reich, the diplomat Hans Thomsen.

Tommy, as the ladies called him, was also of Norwegian parentage, very handsome and charming. He was employed by the German Foreign Office wherever or whenever the more acceptable face of Nazism was required, but could be a tough servant of the Reich if necessary. At this period he was attached to Hitler's Chancellery as the Führer's personal link with visitors from abroad. Subsequently he was sent to Washington and was chargé d'affaires there in the two years before Pearl Harbor. His efforts to keep America out of the war until then were rewarded with the Knight's Cross of the Iron Cross, normally bestowed for feats of exceptional gallantry. He finished up as German ambassador in Stockholm.

Brigitta herself disliked the regime and felt uncomfortable under it. When both the Games and her Wintergarten engagement were over, and there was still no news of *On Your Toes*, she was delighted by Edward's proposal of a motor tour through Italy. What's more, he invited her mother along too. They took the train to Innsbruck, where Edward met them with his Bentley and his chauffeur and his secretary. They went to Verona and Florence and, of course, Ravello. Edward was amused, whenever they met anyone he knew, by the way Brigitta took pains to mention her mother ('My mother who is with us, you know'), as if this made the *ménage* respectable. In fact, it almost certainly was respectable. In her autobiography *Zorina* (New York: Farrar, Straus, Girouard), Brigitta – or Vera – says only nice things about Edward, but adds that she doesn't think women were his persuasion.

September turned into October. They went to Paestum, Pompeii, Capri and then back to Paris, where they put up at the Ritz and Edward sent Brigitta to Schiaparelli. On the strength of news that her musical was finally going ahead, she ordered a midnight-blue evening dress with matching cape, a black woollen jacket and a pink silk evening jacket edged with glass flowers. *On Your Toes* opened at the Coliseum in the new year. It was not a hit in London, but Vera Zorina – as she was now to be permanently – was chosen for the movie version that Sam Goldwyn was planning. She sailed for America to work on the film with Balanchine, who fell in love with, and in due course married, her. For Edward the romance, as he liked to put it (with an odd short 'o'), had hardly been one to scorch these pages, but perhaps it was just what he needed.

Zorina seemed set for a glittering film career. *On Your Toes* was followed by *The Goldwyn Follies*, *Louisiana Purchase* and *Follow the Boys*. Then she fell victim to Hollywood at its cruellest and most cold-blooded. She took a screen test for the part of Maria in *For Whom the Bell Tolls*, was awarded the role with maximum publicity, had her hair cropped, went on location and after two weeks was abruptly dropped in favour of Ingrid Bergman. The marriage with Balanchine also failed. She survived somehow, bravely resumed a career in the theatre and was married again, to the chairman of Columbia Records, Goddard Lieberson. Edward and she always kept in touch.

14

According to Salvador Dalí's biography he met
Edward James for the first time in 1935. Edward's
recollection implied a somewhat earlier date. He
said he was still married to Tilly and staying with a
friend of hers in Spain, the painter José Maria Sert.
When Edward kept on enthusing about Dalí's
work, Sert offered to take him along the coast, by
boat, to meet his hero. At all events, Edward
extended his usual impulsive hand of friendship,
and apparently the two men did get on very well.
Edward used to tell a long and not particularly
edifying story about a train journey from Spain to
Ravello, with Dalí and his beloved Gala. They
became regular guests at the Villa Cimbrone. Also
aboard the train was Edward's then secretary, a
prim English-woman already bemused by this
mad Spaniard and his garden dotted with grotesque sculpture.

Gala had gone to the restaurant car. Through
the open window of the compartment Edward
and Dalí saw a church with a weathercock aloft,
turning in the breeze. At this moment the church
clock chimed six. By a species of telepathy, says

Edward, they simultaneously crowed cocka-doodledoo with straight faces, and repeated the performance on the hour, every hour, for the rest of the journey. Two years later Edward overheard the secretary entertaining friends to tea in her flat at the top of the Wimpole Street house. She was saying, 'This you *won't* believe, but he crows at me in the train, he and his friend.'

Dalí was three years older than Edward. After art school he experimented with various styles, conventionally enough; pointilliste in 1923, cubist in 1924, a Vermeer-like realism in 1925. A land-scape of 1926 introduced an air of mystery for the first time. By 1928 he was a thoroughgoing surrea-list, though not officially accepted into the move-ment until 1934. He will forever be associated in the popular image with droopy watches draped over leafless branches against a deserted seashore background (the actual picture containing all these elements was 'The Persistence of Memory', 1931) or, as Edward's friend Lord Berners put it,

On the pale yellow sands there's a pair of
   clasped hands,
And an eyeball entangled in string
And a bicycle seat and a plate of raw meat,
And a thing that is hardly a thing.

More than any other surrealist painter (which is what completed his appeal for Edward) he acted out the role of surrealist painter, with his pre-posterous moustaches, flamboyant appearance loud pronouncements, staged happenings and

85

public proclamations, such as the 1939 'Declaration of the Independence of the Imagination and the Rights of Man to His Own Madness'. A passionate love life with his model, chatelaine and wife Gala, whom he once said he loved more than his mother or his father or his idol Picasso – yea, even more than he loved money – added the last touch to the picture.

In 1936 Dalí was booked to deliver a lecture at the International Surrealist Exhibition in London. He attempted to do so from inside a diving suit, nearly asphyxiated and stayed at Wimpole Street afterwards to recover. There he and Edward planned a surrealist dinner party in such deplorable taste, in every sense of the word, that it seems just as well that it evidently never took place. The table centrepiece was to have consisted of dwarfs holding candelabra which, at a given signal, they were supposed to raise or lower. The dwarfs proved too difficult to drill to Dalí's standards and the idea was abandoned, together with the proposed menu of oysters ostensibly chilled in ice but actually smoking hot and sitting on hot rock salt, followed by fish-skins stuffed with sirloin steak, potato jackets containing pease pudding and carrots masquerading as peas.

In 1938 the two of them had a celebrated meeting with the surrealists' spiritual father, Sigmund Freud, who had fled Hitler's Austria and was living in St John's Wood, London. Another refugee, the writer Stefan Zweig, had read *The Gardener Who Saw God* and was particularly impressed, he told Edward, by the account of the vision. Would he like to meet the great interpreter of dreams with a view to writing a book about him? The way to go about it would be to be analysed by Freud oneself. Edward took along Dalí and Dalí took along his 'Metamorphosis of Narcissus', which Edward owned, a hand bedded in a spectral landscape with ants crawling up the thumb. Freud studied it for some time and then said only, 'Warum die Ameisen?' – 'Why the ants?' Dalí made sketches that yielded a pair of famous ink portraits of the old man, with his head spiralled like a snail's shell. Freud told Zweig that he had never seen such an archetypal Spaniard, what a fanatic! Edward found himself the onlooker and never pursued the analysis or the book.

All the while he had ben acquiring Dalís, from great canvases like 'The Metamorphosis of Narcissus' and 'Autumn Cannibalism' to a little, but much-prized, extemporization when Edward once spluttered ink from his fountain pen on to a sheet of clean blotting paper and Dalí said, 'Give me that,' and proceeded to turn it into a little landscape with a hill, vineyards, butterflies and sailing ships on the sea. Now, worried because he thought Dalí was dissipating his energy into too many pot-boilers to pay for his (and Gala's) increasingly extravagant mode of life, he struck an extraordinary deal with the painter. If Dalí would concentrate only on more heartfelt works, he would guarantee to buy a year's output (with a minimum of one large painting, one small and ten drawings) at a price which would give Dalí the income he needed. Whether this was an act of inspired patronage or simply an investor protecting his investment is hard to say, because war intervened, and although Edward was already in America and Dalí reached there in 1940, the fruits of the deal had to be left in France and fell into the hands of the Germans. Edward eventually recovered only two of the twelve works, one of them having been melodramatically saved – complete with bullet hole – from the last trainload of loot heading for the Reich.

He had nevertheless amassed a fantastic collection of Dalí's output from long before the old fraud started to sign his name to anything. The great Dalí exhibition of 1970–71 in Rotterdam was actually designated 'Exposition Dalí, avec la collection de Edward F.W. James'. No less than twenty-three oils and eleven ink or wash drawings were acknowledged either to him personally or to the Edward James Foundation.

15

Soon after coming in to West Dean in 1932 Edward had begun to wonder if the big house wasn't too big and too ugly, as well as expensive to run. John Piper suggested that he strip off the Wyatt battlements and flints to regain a classic Georgian house. Instead, he planned to let West Dean House and make Mr Willie's shooting lodge, Monkton House, his country home. Egged on by his artist cronies, he set out to create the first surrealist abode. Dalí designed a famous pair of sofas in the shape of Mae West's lips. Tchelitchew suggested the dark blue and yellow décor of the study when Edward appeared one morning in a dark-blue suit with a cowslip in his buttonhole. Kit Nicholson was the architect and Norris Wakefield the interior decorator, but the final effect of a mad potentate's private brothel, furnished with extravagant jokes, treasures and *kitsch* from every period, was Edward's and Edward's alone.

To seal the outrage for those ready to be outraged, the original lodge (built 1902) was by Sir Edwin Lutyens, the admired architect of small country houses in enlightened folksy style. Edward disliked Monkton's mousy good taste as much as its cottagey little windows, the damp and cold he found there and the memories the place held for him of being bundled thither whenever West Dean itself was given over to a grand party.

Mrs Willie had already added an excrescence to the design in the form of a bathroom. Edward had no compunction about adding another for the sake of symmetry. He made the upstairs windows seem a little more assertive by underhanging them with plaster mouldings in the shape of sheets hung out to air. He replaced what he considered were ugly iron down-pipes with mock-bamboo ones salvaged from St Dunstan's House in Regent's Park when the heiress Betty Hutton was pulling it down. He flanked the front door with two full-sized palm trees carved from wood, an idea he borrowed from a rococo pavilion he'd once seen in southern Germany. The fine brick-work in Tudor herring-bone patterns that Lutyens loved so much – nine-tenths of it he had rendered in cement and, when he decided that white did not harmonize with the surrounding woodlands, sought to paint it the colour of copper beeches instead. All that survived of poor Sir Edwin by the time Mr Edward had finished was one cloister still in bare herring-bone brick.

From West Dean, Monkton is reached by a private road that Willie James built in order to take his guests shooting by new-fangled motor car. It is still known as 'the motor road'. It passes by fields and farms, and through a beech wood. The initial view of the house is end-on, nestling among

West Dean House in 1890, the year Willie James acquired the estate.
Edward James Foundation

The interior of West Dean House, looking along the west corridor. The polar bear was shot on an Arctic expedition of the three brothers. Edward gave it to Dali. *Edward James Foundation*

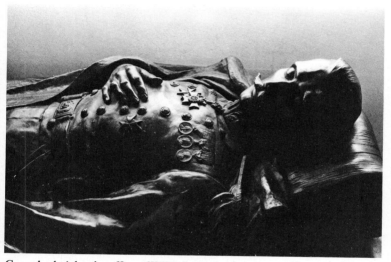

Crusader knight: the effigy of Willie James by Goscombe John, 1917, West Dean church. *Richard Ault*

Edward in a sailor suit, aged about seven.
Edward James Foundation

Tilly Losch as photographed by Hoppé, who liked hands, *c.* 1930.
Mansell Collection

Pavel Tchelitchew's drawing for the jacket of *The Gardener Who Saw God*, c. 1937. *Edward James Foundation*

for Robert
from Edward
17 years before we met

Photograph of Edward James for *The Bones of My Hand* jacket
by Yevondé, *c.* 1937. *Edward James Foundation*

Monkton House, photographed for the 1986 sale. *Pereds*

the trees. When I glimpsed it for the first time in 1977, I thought how small the place looked, though in fact it has six bedrooms, four or five downstairs rooms, usual offices. My second re-action was the usual one of shock and disbelief at its colour; if Edward's attempt to match the colour of copper beeches had ever been successful, it had by now turned to a blotchy purple. But the carved palm trees on each side of the door, rotted by forty years of damp, had lately been replaced by dur-able fibreglass simulacra moulded from the originals.

In the garden was a newly built peacock roosting house, with pillars to the same palm-tree conceit, to house the creatures that represented Edward's later-life passion for rare and usually smelly birds. There were statues whose modesty was preserved by natural draperies of ivy, a wartime air-raid shelter converted into a sauna bath, loudspeakers on the roof, which used to blast wireless music in Edward's direction when he was gardening. I craned my neck to see the chimney-clock that told the day of the week, not the hour of day.

Inside – inside it was Tutankhamun's tomb, the Sleeping Beauty's palace, the ghost train out of season. The rooms were shuttered, sound was muffled, a musky smell hung in the air, for against the imagined cold and damp all those years before, Edward or Norris Wakefield had decided to quilt all the interior walls with silk and worsted. It proved a promised land for moths, so every six months experts came to let off chemical bombs. Because of the risk of burglary, the windows were seldom opened and the smell had never quite cleared away. I picked my way through the gloom, past shrouded furniture and unpacked crates and stacks of pictures, moved out of West Dean House in 1970 or retrieved from Wimpole Street thirty years before that, and still waiting to be sorted out.

There was a standard lamp made from a boa-constrictor shot by Uncle Frank before the elephant got him; another lamp made by the surrealist sculptor Giacometti, glass with ivy twined around. Dominating the hall was the Delvaux 'Les Belles de Nuit', the eye led willy-nilly to the pubic thicket – formidable even by Delvaux standards – sported by the principal belle, though tough competition came from the outstretched human arms, said to be those of a drowning man, which formed the back of the hall chair in front of the painting. In the sitting room I peered under dust sheets at one of Dalí's Mae West sofas. There was a Dalí on the wall too, 'Le Pharmacien d'Ampurdan ne cherchant absolument rien', no less, oil on board, 30 by 52 cm, No. 48 in that definitive Amsterdam catalogue. In the blue and yellow study, the room inspired by Edward's suit and cowslip buttonhole, was a Eugène Berman *trompe-l'oeil* pretending to be a bit of old marble column, to which two scruffy drawings had been tacked. Somewhere or elsewhere, unless I'm dreaming it, lurked Leonor Fini's *après*-orgy 'Figures on a Terrace'.

The curving staircase which replaced Lutyens's original square one might have been filched from

the nearest Odeon. Half-way up there was supposed to be an aquarium and also a window into
the side of someone's bath; I forgot to look for
either. The green stair-carpet, together with areas
of floor carpet, was patterned with doggy paw-
prints. Edward used to claim a functional reason
for having it thus woven – against such a design,
natural muddy paw-marks wouldn't show up. But
he must also have been cocking a snook at Tilly, in
which case Tilly had some small revenge; her
carpet in West Dean had been worked out so
carefully on graph paper that even on a spiral
staircase the footprints fell only on the treads.
Here, the paw-prints occurred indiscriminately on
risers and treads alike.

Upstairs, the bedroom opened off a strange
windowless corridor. The doors were covered
with the same stuff as the walls, which made them
hard to spot at first. The Ivy Room had ivy
wallpaper and ivy motifs everywhere. Edward's
room had a four-poster whose posts, like the
front-door guardians and peacock-house pillars,
were carved as palm trees. His bathroom had a
domed alabaster ceiling, an alabaster window and
an alabaster wall that lit up with sun and moon
effects. In the Green Bathroom, off the Green
Bedroom, a sunken mirror rose sluggishly at the
touch of a button, and the medicine cabinet was
disguised as a bookcase full of books. In every
room the wastepaper and laundry bins were made
of flimsy metal, printed with facsimiles of *Life*
magazine covers whose dates there was no need
to stoop and read. They were all 1937, the year

Edward moved in, if ever he did move in.

Downstairs again, the Map Room was so called because one entire wall was covered by an enormous map. It was not of the world, nor of Europe, nor even of Italy, where Edward always claimed to have been happiest. It was a map of Spain, where that same year the civil war was capturing everyone's attention. Only in the big kitchen warmed by a pair of Aga cookers, where the caretakers made tea and ate their sandwiches, did Monkton House impart any feeling of having been lived in. For the rest, it was a museum – or mausoleum – to the world of Edward James of forty years before.

16

About this time Edward's urge for self-expression led him also to a flirtation with popular journalism, in the person of Lord Beaverbook. Since he knew everyone and was forever telling amusing stories about them, might he not be of some use to the *Evening Standard* and *Daily Express*? The arrangement did not work out entirely satisfactorily – Edward remembered being summoned to Beaverbrook's suite in the Ritz in Paris and told that his style was far too flowery, too literary. 'Why can't you write the story like you told it to me over the dinner table last night?' growled Beaverbrook, and taking up the trumpet mouthpiece of his famous Dictaphone he recorded instructions to be relayed to Fleet Street: 'The following information will be added to Mr James's article . . .'

But there was one notable triumph. Edward had sub-let the Villa Cimbrone for a few weeks to Greta Garbo, who arrived there, to the excitation of the world's gossip columnists, with Leopold Stokowski. From privileged information gathered from his servants, Edward was able to disclose that far from being romantic lovers, the two slept in opposite wings of the villa, and their intimacy was confined to calisthenics on the lawn, during which Garbo had been heard to reprove the great musician, 'Vun, two, three, four – Mr Stokowski, can you not keep time?' Edward later expanded the story into a *New Yorker* piece which appeared above a pen-name he had lately borrowed from West Dean's former owners, 'Edward Selsey'.

His poetic output had meanwhile continued steadily. *Minotaure*'s issue No. 8, in 1936, carried a trio of surrealist poems, *Les Trois Sécheresses* (*The Three Droughts*) with illustrations by Dalí, which were later set to music by Poulenc. His self-publishing also continued. Though it bore Duckworth's imprint, *So Far So Glad* appeared only in a private limited edition. The text, a painfully jocular prose romance featuring a Princess Frigidaire, allusions to advertising fads of the day and even a reference to Jew-baiting in Nazi Germany, was the first to be ascribed to Edward Selsey. The James Press was reborn for this same author's *Rich Man, Poor Man, Beggarman, Wop* (1937–8), a nondescript collection of letters, whimsy, verse and a long story about Mussolini's dog which arbitrarily breaks off and is resumed in a subsequent volume, *Propaganda an International Dog*. Again it is a good idea – the dog eventually meets Mrs Chamberlain's Pekinese and helps effect a détente – but the writing is incredibly discursive, ill-organized and sententious. After fifty years the volumes still have the smell and feel of a rich man's self-indulgence, with their fine binding, gold-decked paper, bizarre typography, coloured punctuation marks, indiscriminate use of illustrations, and prevailing archness. Magritte's picture of the back of Edward's head is used both times as a frontispiece (with wildly differing colour reproduction). 'The author's reflexion illudes him in the mirror,' the caption to the first reads, '– Portrait of Mr Selsey by R.M.' The pretentious spelling, the arch anonymity that is not anonymity, say it all. What could a struggling author truly at risk have made of such a production? For that matter, what did the luckless friends and relatives showered with copies make of it?

But then came *The Bones of My Hand*. This was something different again: Edward's final and carefully considered bid for recognition as a poet. It was published by the Oxford University Press, though subsidized by Edward (unfortunately, as things turned out) in his usual lavish style. For half a guinea the volume included a frontispiece by Tchelitchew, the score of a song of Edward's set to music by Henri Sauguet and on the wrapper an impressive camera portrait, in colour, of the author. The hundred or so pages of verse include some early work reprinted, including 'La Belle au Bois Dormant', a rapturous version of the Sleeping Beauty fairy story. From one of Tilly's illnesses comes 'To a Young Woman under Chloroform':

Get well, dear love! Get strong with all the strength
   that feeds upon the beauty of your self,
and I will through the gardens of the hills

lead you, my white doe, upwards to the
brink . . .

From his year at West Dean comes perhaps the
most interesting poem in the collection, 'Shut
Gates', about an old *seigneur* (perhaps a vision of
how Edward saw himself in the far-off future)
who has withdrawn from the world behind the
locked gates of his estate:

'My mother despised me, And I would blush.
'And that was so terribly long ago.
'My wife is still lovely, they say – but hush!
'She was lovely, lovely, lovely, I know.
'They want my money, they want my blood.
'They've had my love but they've spewed it out.
'They've envied my pictures, my farms, my stud.
'Keep them out: keep them out: keep them
    out. . .'

The accumulated resentments and disappoint-
ments of a lifetime came spilling forth, and most of
all the disappointment of the children that never
lived, the resentment of love that turned to hatred.
The old man waits for death. Edward was not
thirty when he wrote it. Alas, the volume that
contained it contained also the makings of a last
blow. *The Bones of My Hand* was published early
in 1938 to respectful, even glowing notices in the
Evening Standard, the *Times Literary Supplement* and *John O'London's*. But in the *New
Statesman* Stephen Spender delivered an attack
that in Edward's soured memory stopped him

from ever publishing again. 'Mr Edward James,' he would tell you the notice went, 'owns great wealth, several houses, a Rolls-Royce, a yacht. He seems to think that he can also buy himself a reputation as a poet.'

What Spender in fact wrote was both milder and more devious. Entrusted with the review of five different volumes of poetry (under the heading 'Grocer's Wine') he proposed dealing with them in order of seriousness: precedence went to an anthology whose contributors included Lawrence Durrell and Rayner Heppenstall '... and last place to wit, wealth, beauty, travel, possessions, charm, grace and sensibility, all showered in eightiesh [sic] profusion on Mr Edward James, but owing, alas, for their expression, more to the photographer of his portrait on the cover; to Mr Tchelitcheff, draughtsman of his *three* hands, one with bones, one giving, perhaps, the Nazi salute, one giving, indubitably, the clenched fist in the frontispiece; and to the red, black and ornamental type setter of the Oxford University Press, than to the muse of Mr James himself.'

Edward never noticed what might have been some consolation: next-to-last place above him went to Hilaire Belloc.

17

As Europe stumbled towards war in 1938, then shrank back at Munich, Edward was on a hilarious motor tour of Yugoslavia and Albania with a figure from the past now married to Iris Tree, the giant Count Friedrich Ledebur. They had many escapades involving frontier guards and nights in prison, and Edward grew the little Vandyke beard he was to sport thereafter. In at least one photograph of him taken on his return, it has to be said, the result makes him look remarkably like the English cult comedian of the 1970s, Kenny Everett, but the only reaction Edward himself recalled was the woman passer-by who shrieked at him, 'I suppose you think you're very clever.'

The following winter, Edward accompanied Dalí to New York on what was to be a last surrealist adventure before war broke out. Dalí had been commissioned to dress a window for Bonwit Teller, the plush Fifth Avenue store; he was also going to devise an extravagant spectacle at the World's Fair, with Edward putting up 48 per cent of the capital. The window display, inspired by Botticelli's 'Venus' consisted essentially of a female wax dummy arising from a tin bath filled with narcissi: though it was perfectly innocuous, the crowds it drew were enough to alarm the Bonwit Teller management. Dalí's Gala happened to pass by as they were furtively modifying the tableau. In the fierce row that ensued, Edward tried to negotiate a civilized settlement, pointing out that if the company wished to have Dalí's name it had also to respect his integrity. Meanwhile the artist chose to resolve matters there and then by storming into the window, lifting the bath tub on high and hurling it through the plate glass. He stepped out into Fifth Avenue after it, a second before the rest of the window could collapse on him, spent some hours in jail, but made his point. It was also useful publicity for the other venture.

Edward was much more involved in this, both as a backer and, in the inevitable last-minute exposition panic to get it ready, as unpaid clerk of works and general factotum. The New York World's Fair was one of the worst-timed festivities in history, enjoying a few months' frenetic gaiety in the summer of 1939, then dragging on for another year while the countries it was supposed to be bringing together in fun and harmony were either at each other's throats or very soon to be so. As well as serious national and commercial pavilions it had a lusty fun-fair element. At the World's Fair Americans saw their first television, and many of them their first striptease and fan-dancers.

Respectability could be added to the latter attractions by bringing in an artist's name. Pavel

Tchelitchew designed a World's Fair routine for the great stripper Gipsy Rose Lee. Dalí called his contribution 'The Dream of Venus', Venus evidently being on his mind that year. It was an underwater surrealist spectacle housed in a palace of fake coral bearing a twenty-five-foot-high reproduction of Botticelli's goddess. Inside was a vast L-shaped tank with plate-glass windows thirty feet by twenty feet. Inside that was a backdrop depicting an underwater Pompeii with such Dalí-esque props as a door with a zip fastener down the centre, a typewriter like seaweed and a piano in the shape of a woman's corpse, all fashioned from the synthetic rubber whose manufacturers were partly sponsoring the show. The great attraction, however, came from the mermaids who swam in and out of the setting in long shocking-pink gloves and divided tails executed in the same synthetic rubber but, at first, with bare breasts. When some of the gamier side-shows started to overstep the mark, and a 'clean up the World's Fair' campaign ensued, they had to wear seaweed tops, and attendances fell off. Edward believed the real fault was the timidity of the backers, which resulted in Dalí's concept being 'Disneyfied'; the public had better taste than the entrepreneurs would allow; the crowds were always thickest and most attentive at the parts of the spectacle which remained closest to Dalí's intention. Dalí himself had veered off to the Metropolitan Opera House to stage a ballet. Edward sold his share in the 'Dream' and might have returned to Europe had not an entirely different circumstance detained him.

The immensely rich Arthur Curtis James was obviously approaching the end of his life. He had no children of his own. Though Edward was strictly his cousin – they were both grandsons of Daniel James – the great difference in their ages always made the relationship seem one of uncle and nephew. 'Aunt' Harriet sent for Edward and put it to him that it was, however, by no means certain that he would inherit all, or even any, of the railroad and mining and timber millions. The old man had become increasingly xenophobic over the years. Perhaps other members of the family had been murmuring things in his ear. Certainly Tilly had been to see him during the break-up of her marriage with Edward. Whatever the cause, he had taken against the English branch of the family and against Edward in particular. As a first step towards a reconciliation it might be a very good idea if Edward thought about becoming an American citizen. Edward obediently filed his first citizenship papers.

This, at least, was Edward's story. It is not difficult to think of an alternative explanation, that with war clouds so obviously gathering in Europe the impulse was one to save his skin. But naturalization wasn't an essential to remaining in America. Many Britons spent half their lives there without becoming United States citizens, and in the event Edward never pursued his application. He travelled all his life on a British passport. Arthur Curtis James died in due course and according to Edward left his millions to charities;

not even to very useful charities, he used to add sourly. In fact, some money did go to the English branch of the family.

Another inducement to linger on in America arose from Edward's friendship with Tchelitchew, who was by now an American citizen and firmly established on the New York gallery scene. He and Charles Henri Ford still lived together, and Edward was presumably no fonder of Charles Henri. But in the second of his post-Tilly romantic attachments he fell for the beautiful young man's beautiful sister Ruth, an aspirant actress. Tchelitchew, needless to say, had painted her portrait. Edward, needless to say, acquired it; it showed a ravishing girl with long dark hair falling from a centre parting, huge eyes, her left arm across her breast, her right hand clutching the blanket swathed around her. Behind her, for no obvious reason, disembodied hands spelled her name in sign language.

Charles Henri expected Edward and her to marry. 'They are like that,' he wrote to Parker Tyler, another friend of Tchelitchew's and his future biographer (*The Divine Comedy of Pavel Tchelitchew*, Weidenfeld & Nicolson, 1969). Edward sought to foster her career in his usual manner. He introduced her to Orson Welles, whose Mercury Theatre company had scored a great success in New York with a modern-dress production of *Julius Caesar*, not to mention the radio version of *War of the Worlds* which drove thousands into a panic. Ruth's eyes, however, were on Hollywood. She was taken on by one of

104

the studios as a 'starlet', and although Edward continued to see her when he also moved to California, she eventually married another man. It was to prove an unhappy and short-lived match; in due course she was married again, to Zachary Scott the actor, and in the 1940s and 1950s achieved a name for herself in the theatre, notably in Faulkner's *Requiem for a Nun*.

In later life, still a remarkably handsome woman, she dearly wished to acquire the Tchelitchew portrait of herself. Before he died, Zachary Scott made several attempts. Edwards was sympathetic but said that the painting was no longer his to offer. It belonged now to the Edward James Foundation. There may have been, as some American friends suspected, an element of wilfulness in this. Edward could be very generous if the thought was his own but often appeared to take a perverse satisfaction in denying anyone who too plainly sought something. 'She wanted it too bad,' the friends said. But Ruth herself always believed that Edward wished her to have the picture, and the story had a happy ending. When the Foundation put it up for auction at Christie's, London, in the summer of 1990, Miss Ford made the successful bid by letter; the portrait now hangs in her apartment in the Dakota building in New York.

Once more Edward felt flat and emptied. London and Ravello seemed very far away. Monkton House was fun, but it was complete now, there was nothing left to do. His literary career lay in ruins, thanks to Stephen Spender. Why go back? In a sense, he never did.

18

What first led him to California, Edward used to say, was an interest in mysticism that had been growing in him ever since that vision of creation in the dining room at West Dean. There were reports of a remarkable Vedanta movement, derived from Hindu faiths, that flourished in Los Angeles under the tutelage of the legendary Krishnamurti. Many of its devotees were drawn from the writers and artists of the Hollywood film colony; an active prophet seemed to be an Englishman, Gerald Heard. Edward had been impressed by Heard's book *Pain, Sex and Time*. Another attraction was that the Aldous Huxleys, who had arrived in Hollywood with Heard in 1938, were bound to be involved, and Edward was also much swayed at this time by *Ends and Means*, a pacifist and philosophical analysis of the world's ills that Aldous had just published. He flung himself into the Vedanta circle with characteristic enthusiasm. He became a disciple of the Swami Prabhavan-andra. He attended Gerald Heard's lectures at the Vedanta Temple. He lived a simple life, meditated for the prescribed hours, abstained from alchohol and when lunching with the Huxleys in their favourite Farmer's Market restaurant (not then the tourist attraction it became in more knowing times), would nibble at the same vegetarian nuts and salads, though not without a certain awareness of the absurd posturing. He told a story of how he took Ruth Ford there one day for a *tête-à-tête*. The Huxleys were already at table with Rosalind Rajagopal, the wife of one of Krishnamurti's associates. Aldous insisted they join them, though Maria Huxley was obviously less keen. She was, according to Edward, a natural snob who had been weaned away from social and even intellectual snobbery by Aldous's gentle example, but had become instead a spiritual snob. A little Warner Brothers starlet was clearly out of her depth in such company. Edward overheard her whisper to Mrs Rajagopal, 'My dear, I fear the poor girl is not yet past the first stage of purgation!'

More hurtful was the attitude of Gerald Heard, an eloquent preacher but a figure whose reputation seems otherwise to decline with every new memoir of the period. 'What can Huxley' – or Krishnamurti or Prabhavanandra – 'have seen in him?' is a constant refrain. Heard viewed Edward's mysticism with the prejudice which had blighted every other calling he pursued: how could a *millionaire* be serious about meditation? Discouraged, Edward gradually drifted away, but kept up some of the friendships he had made. There was Christopher Isherwood, for example, and through Isherwood a whole spreading homosexual circle with its own intriguing buzz of gossip and scandal and sulking and scheming. And there was what might be called the Ojai connection. Ojai, a little community up the coast towards Santa Barbara, was a kind of Mecca to the Hollywood Vedantists, a spiritual retreat. It was also where a wandering theatrical troupe led by Michael Tchekhov, grandson of the dramatist, had settled when war prevented their return to Europe, and where in due course a festival theatre arose. One of the players was Edward's old friend Iris Tree, daughter of the Victorian romantic actor Beerbohm Tree, sister of Viola Tree, and Tilly's predecessor as the nun in *The Miracle*. A very young member of the company was Daphne Moore, also from England, whom we will meet again as Daphne Field. Ojai's latter-day fame, or notoriety, as the home town of the heroine of television's *Bionic Woman* derived not from this theatrical association, incidentally, but from the fact that the producer of that series, Lee Siegel, had married the daughter of one of the Vedanta temple maidens.

At the same time Edward moved in the exalted circles his wealth and family connections commanded for him. His first hostess in Hollywood was Peggy Bok Kiskadden, its uncrowned queen and arch-lionizer, descended from one, if not two, of the founding fathers of the republic. Through her he met the movie stars: Bette Davis, Ronald Colman, Humphrey Bogart. Equally, there was the growing community of European refugees settling in the film capital for the duration, many of whom he had met in happier times: the

Stravinskys, the Darius Milhauds, Thomas Mann, Heinrich Mann, Bruno Frank, Lion Feuchtwanger, Carl Zuckmayer, eventually even Salvador Dalí...

It must have been an idyllic place then. The smog had not yet started to accumulate in the stagnant pool of air between the mountains and the ocean which today encloses Los Angeles in a more or less permanent blur. The sky was a bright blue, the lines of the terrain sharp against it. The studio lots sprawled over hundreds of acres, workplaces where they started early in the morning, yes, but finished early and tranquilly as well, with drinks on the lawn. The residential areas of Beverly Hills and Brentwood Park were still separated by tracts of scrub. Sunset Boulevard wound its way through the mansions of the rich to Pacific Palisades and the coast road to the stars' beach houses at Malibu. Red tramcars shuttled along centre tracks now grassed over and trodden daily by joggers.

Edward rented houses, at first in Beverly Hills and then at Laguna Beach, a long way down from central Los Angeles but traditionally something of an artists' quarter and also chosen by Gerald Heard for his 'prayer centre'. Edward's sister Sylvia went to live there later, along with various pets, and stayed until she died in the 1980s. Edward would have liked to buy his house, but already the usual conspiracies were intervening. Friends who should have told him it was for sale neglected to do so; a speculator bought it and asked him double the price; and though it would still have been a bargain, it was 'psychologically impossible' for him to pay up. He sacrificed the fitted carpets he had just laid and settled, in so far as he ever settled anywhere, at 6707 Milner Road, Hollywood, towards the crest of the Hollywood Hills. Like many of the houses built on steep hillsides or canyon edges, it was deceptive. From the road it looked modest in size, but cut into the slope were as many floors below the entrance level as there were above it.

Edward found a Swedish cook whose breathtaking ignorance charmed him. When the sun set, did it go to China, perhaps? Or Canada? Or did it become the moon? – no, she'd sometimes seen the sun and moon at the same time. He bought a car, a Mercury, and engaged as chauffeur one of the Ojai actors, Woodrow Chambliss. He began what was to become the ever more frequent, ever more tortuous, ever more speculative process of finding a secretary – no, not just a secretary; the *right* secretary. He resumed the writing of poetry, even if he wasn't going to publish it. He endeavoured to supervise his affairs in England with volleys of cables and letters. He entertained, he cultivated. In short, he constructed round himself again the perpetual-motion machine whose only purpose was its own activity.

Meanwhile the German armies overran Europe, the U-boat packs ravaged Atlantic shipping, and in December 1941 the Japanese attacked Pearl Harbor. However distant from these happenings in actual miles, Hollywood was very conscious of them. The sound stages of MGM and 20th-Century Fox and Paramount and Universal echoed to the noise of battle as Dunkirk, Dieppe, Bataan and Corregidor were reconstructed. Familiar figures departed for the real thing, some failing to return. The question has to be asked, what did Edward do in the war, and the answer has to be 'nothing'. Indeed it could be said that his chief concern, as the heavens were falling, was how to get sufficient funds out of beleaguered Britain. The bad news of Arthur Curtis's will had just reached him (actually while on a trip to Texas). His capital in England was frozen under emergency exchange regulations. For a while the only income to reach him was the rent he was paid for Binderton House, a little Queen Anne manor house on the West Dean estate that was let during the war – and this was perhaps why the money got through – to Anthony Eden, then foreign secretary.

Edward was eligible for service in the American armed forces, he said, but classified 4-F at his medical because of his boyhood intestinal operation and subsequent history of ulcers. He also had a crooked toe. He tried for the Allied Monuments Commission, formed to follow the armies, especially in Italy, with the aim of safeguarding art and architectural treasures, but was turned down. He was in line, later, for a mission to the Chungking government in China that was going to help organize industry; someone else had more pull. What makes his version of events rather easier to accept than might otherwise be the case is that he could, if he had chosen to, have enjoyed a spurious reputation as a secret agent.

Before gasoline rationing began to limit his

travels, he made many mysterious journeys down towards the Mexican border and who-knew-what destinations beyond. Woodie Chambliss would drive him in the Mercury as far as Tucson or even El Paso. There Edward would board a plane with brief instructions as to which airport and when he was to be met. Woodie would turn up at the appointed hour, wait in vain, and go back day after day at the same time until one day – or night – Edward would step off the DC-3 and climb into the car just as if this had been the precise arrangement. Rumour persists that he was some kind of Ashenden, but to do him justice, Edward scoffed at the idea. All he was doing was to indulge a boyish delight in travel and flying, to give a fresh whirl to the perpetual-motion machine. Once when Woodie met him off a plane in the early hours of the morning, he insisted on being driven fifty miles to Manby Springs near Taos in New Mexico, where D. H. Lawrence's widow Frieda (whom Edward knew, of course) had a ranch. Under the moonlight in a lonely field a puddle of muddy hot water gently seethed. It was, said Edward, a natural spring regarded by local Indians as having supernatural properties, and he had just bought it; stripping off his clothes, he slithered into the water there and then. Edward retained this curious little property until he died, paying $15 land tax on it every year. His estate finally sold it to the American Monument Trust.

In 1942 his passion switched to the giant red-wood forests of northern California. There he travelled with an unnamed male companion and completed – or completed for the time being – the sequence of amatory sonnets he called *For the Lonely*, among them the one in which he was trying to lay the ghost of Tilly. They were printed for private circulation only, with a preface which put the war firmly in its place: '. . . however universal that disaster may be at this moment, it is after all only a topical incident of history which must pass, whereas loneliness and grief are constants to humanity which even an Utopia could not banish . . .'

Edward did nevertheless make one quirky contingency plan should the worse come to worst and the Japanese invade. He bought a printing press (after all, an old love) and installed it in the bottommost basement at Milner Road, ready to turn out resistance literature. When in 1945–6 the fear of nuclear holocaust became a fashionable obsession, Edward revived and enlarged the idea. Alongside the printing press went copies of all the world's masterpieces of literature – in the event of the unthinkable, the raw materials for an eventual renaissance. That he didn't take the prospect quite as gloomily as, say, Aldous Huxley in his futuristic fable, *Ape and Essence*, is indicated in a story that Edward hatched with Salvador Dalí at this time. Their character was a great collector, perhaps of rare postage stamps. How would he spend the last few hours before the deadly fall-out arrived? They decided that he would go on a frenzied raid of his rivals' hoards – he would know exactly who owned what – and as the Last Trump sounded have, for one moment of utter satisfaction, the absolute collection.

19

With the approach of peace, Edward resumed his travels. There was the momentous 1945 trip to Mexico with the Texan segeant, Roland McKenzie. With the end of the war, there were the first visits back to Europe. Edward stayed at the Ritz in Paris and, because petrol was still scarce there, hired a little pony and carriage with a woman driver. But England, shabby, battered, almost bankrupted by the war and confined to a régime in some respects even more austere than during hostilities, he found depressing. Of his friends, or those he liked to count his friends, Rex Whistler had been killed in Normandy when leading his troop of tanks as an elderly subaltern in the Guards Armoured Division; Basil Ava had been killed in the last days of the Burma campaign. The house in Wimpole Street had been badly damaged in an air-raid, after being let to a refugee couturier whose niece was suspected of being a spy – a story Christopher Sykes adapted for his novel *The Answer to Question 33*. In 1949 Edward sold the property. The ground and first floors became doctors' or dentists' premises, those above were turned into flats. In 1977 it was refurbished again and let to a medical organization which specialized in bringing private patients to London for heart surgery. Only the lift shaft and one unexpectedly luxurious bathroom survived from more eccentric days.

As for West Dean, every available acre had been turned over to food production; the legal publishers Butterworths, evacuated from London, had occupied the stable block. Edward nevertheless lived there again in 1948–9 during what was to be his last sojourn in Britain of any length. He told me about working in the garden of Monkton House to the music, relayed by the rooftop loudspeakers, of the BBC's aloof new Third Programme. According to a rather bilious memoir by Lord Lambton in the *Spectator*, though, he was still quartered in West Dean House and only took his young visitor to Monkton after lunch to show him around.

Writing nearly forty years on (14 June 1986), Lambton recalled Edward as 'a miserable-looking little man with meagre, petulant limbs, a sparse beard, mean face and shifty little eyes'. He also took a keen dislike to Edward's house guests, whoever they may have been; they were 'neither young, pretty nor clever but second-rate, tinselly and on the make, all waiting to laugh or applaud whenever their host spoke'. At Monkton Edward insisted that Lambton should try to play a stone piano in the garden, despite his protestations that he was non-musical. After hitting the stone keys for some time, a trickle of rusty water finally leaked on to Lambton's trousers. 'It's meant to gush!' Edward screamed in fury. 'The whole point is that the water should flow like music.' He went on to blame the gardeners who had let the pipes block up. You couldn't rely on anyone since the war.

Another visit which left sour tastes all round was that of Carlyle Brown, a Californian painter (1920–63) energetically promoted by Tchelitchew and duly patronized by Edward. He arrived with his wife, and in the end they stayed at West Dean for six months. When Edward was absent for a while, something or other happened to produce a quarrel that dragged on, by post, for many months more. Luckily there were some warmer encounters, notably with Dylan Thomas. They met at one of Edith Sitwell's regular lunches, then Edward called on the poet and Caitlin Thomas in Oxford. Later, Dylan sent him one of the pleas for financial assistance which he composed as carefully as – perhaps, more carefully than – his poems. Edward responded with £20 accompanied by a cheerful note. A Dylan Thomas enthusiast and scholar, Chris Zielinski, is convinced that Edward was the inspiration for one if not two of the characters in *The Death of the King's Canary*, an elaborate parody that Thomas wrote with John Davenport, even though this work dates from eight years earlier, 1940–41. Apparently Thomas had been on a famous motor tour of Sussex with John Betjeman and Cyril Connolly and others in 1939. They drove past West Dean, may even have ventured inside to take a look at Monkton House – Edward was in America at the time. Its surrealization would have certainly been a topic of conversation. Zielinski believes that West Dean and Monkton House also feature in the poem as, respectively, the stately home 'Dymmock Hall' and its gatehouse.

What to do with West Dean had been bothering Edward, off and on since he came into the estate at the age of twenty-five. It was the property by which he was identified in Burke's *Landed Gentry*; it had been Willie James's great pride, and he held his father in exaggerated respect. On the other hand, the house itself was a drain on his resources. At one time he had been going to sell it to the Duke of Westminister, another time to the first Lord Camrose, the newspaper peer. From somewhere he hatched a wild idea to make it a distant department of Peking University. Eventually – in 1957 – the house was let to a girls' boarding school, Wispers.

By July 1949 Edward was back in the United States. For tax reasons, all subsequent visits to England were restricted to the number of days allowed by the Inland Revenue and his accountant.

20

Considering how much he hated Los Angeles, or always said he did, it is odd to work out that Edward made it his base for the best part of a quarter of a century. He would vanish for long periods, of course, sending his friends the rambling letters* written in constantly varied coloured inks for which he became renowned. As well as regular visits to Europe, Mexico increasingly attracted him. But sooner or later he would be back in Milner Road, or after Milner Road, Malibu or, more often than not, in the Bel-Air Hotel or one of the Hiltons or even the Holiday Inn, resuming the busy, aimless round as if he had never been away.

* In a letter to Gerald Berners early in 1949 he lists the other people to whom he owes letters: 'Tchelitchew in New York, Sforzino Sforza in Paris, Monroe Wheeler in New Jersey, the sculptor Francesco Coccia and his wife Hilda in Rome, and American sculptor Seymour Fox in Maine, Patrick O'Higgins in New York, Plutarco Gastelum in Mexico, Leonor Fini in Paris, Leonora Carrington in Mexico, Yvonne de Casa Fuerte in Long Island, Florence de Montferrier in Bermuda, Bettina Bergery in Paris, Karl Hofer in Berlin, René Magritte in Brussels and Gaston Bergery in jail . . .'

The hotels were part of the mysterious whirl. Though he always had a home, if not two homes, in the district, he would frequently move into a room in a hotel or apartment house. Sometimes he would continue to sleep at home and have a hotel room for work, or even two rooms for different activities, writing poetry at the Hilton, say, and something else at the Holiday Inn.

Then there were brief local forays to Ojai or Santa Barbara, where Betty Harford, from the Ojai theatre, had settled with her then husband, Oliver Andrews the sculptor. 'Edward would come and spend the weekend with us. He was always great fun, loved gaiety, loved pranks. We'd do crazy things.' And every coming and every going, whether for a day or for six months, meant a ritual of packing and unpacking as legendary as the polychromatic letters. Every article had to be wrapped in tissue paper, preferably pink, and in the case of sets of things, such as the coloured ballpoint pens, the individual items further wrapped and tied with Scotch tape. Once he flew in from Mexico, it is said, with a single suitcase. Inside, a baffled customs officer found only tissue paper wrapped in tissue paper. The converse of this story, told by Paul Millard, a businessman friend, had him arriving for a mere lunch date at Nina Foch's, but choosing to arrive by a helicopter that landed him on the roof of the Rexall drugstore near by and from which, inexplicably, nine pieces of luggage were unloaded.

The tissue was symptomatic of an obsession with cleanliness (or, as some would say, an urge to insulate himself against the world) which manifested itself in other forms. When Edward and his secretary at the time, Joe Le Seur, were working on something of Edward's in the Bel-Air, the room-service waiter brought in lunch once and, to make room for the tray, moved the stack of freshly typed pages. 'You've ruined it,' Edward is supposed to have screamed, until Le Seur calmed him down by undertaking to type the whole thing out again. The secretaries were a saga in themselves. Should he find some promising young writer and give him this opportunity of earning a living, and perhaps even learning a thing or two, while having plenty of time for his own work? Or should he settle for a professional? In the former category were Le Seur, who became a playwright, and Tom Wright and Speed Lamkin and George Bachman and Friedrich Ledebur's son Christopher. Alternating with them were business-like women, among them – improbably – Lauren Bacall's mother and, in New York, the poet Mary Barnard, who put the experience into a literary memoir she published in 1983 called *Assault on Mount Helicon*. The quest for each new candidate was drawn out and agonized. Once the selection had been made, he or she was always the most perfect secretary ever, possessed of unique qualifications and invariably discovered to have some special or co-incidental or even surrealist reason for being Edward's helpmate, such as the same blood-group or birth-stone or fierce dislike of some colour or tune or food. After a brief period of harmony would come the dawning realization that the paragon could not type or spell or accept dictation in Spanish, and was not really qualified at all, and then the equally drawn out and agonized business of disentangling from him or her.

While the relationship lasted, Edward would alternate between extreme generosity and a casual parsimony, omitting to pay the poor secretary until he had to ask for his money and be reminded of his employee status. It was the same with entertaining. In Europe Edward had pre-ferred to do this in his own home. In America he loved restaurant life and was always taking parties to restaurants. Sometimes he would not only stand the meal but bestow handsome gifts on everyone; at the Imperial Garden, a Japanese restaurant, it might be silk kimonos and robes all round. But once, at a beach restaurant in Santa Monica, when the bill came he pretended to have no money with him and waited until his guests had sheepishly emptied their pockets and purses, and still not found enough between them, before discovering a single bedraggled cheque on his person and solving the problem.

Perhaps it was only a flicker of rebellion against the assumption that he was an inexhaustible source of wealth. Or was it that he enjoyed having power over people, stirring things up? Ivan Moffat, who had known him first in England, saw him now as a gadfly forever trying to sting others into joining in his buzzing round, or (with a change of metaphor) as someone needing to enmesh every-one else in layers and layers of activity which in the end accomplished nothing but helped to foster

121

the illusion that he was passing the time industriously. A less than flattering picture begins to emerge, of an impish figure in a well-pressed silk suit, his complexion smooth with an almost brittle smoothness, loving to stir things, rather enjoying mischief for its own sake. He used to enjoy going to homosexual bars late at night, Betty Harford remembered, just to watch the jockeying and desperate pairing off as closing time approached. Certainly he could be either extraordinarily insensitive or extraordinarily dog-in-the-mangerish. When Betty Harford had the lead in a play on in town, *The Candied House*, Edward used to telephone her, or her fellow principal, every night just before the curtain went up, as if wanting to distract them.

Many years earlier, when Woodie Chambliss was his chauffeur and Woodie's wife Erika was about to have their first child, Edward nevertheless made him wait in the car for hours outside the Brown Derby, or wherever it was, until finally Iris Tree stormed downtown and into the restaurant and shamed him into letting Woodie go. When the baby arrived, he was so unobservant that, having seen Erika breast-feeding the child many times, his present to her was a bottle sterilizer. 'We turned it in,' Woodie told me, 'for Beethoven's Sixth on records.'

It might be put forward in diffident mitigation that Edward was off the top layer of an ordered society in which (according to a neat encapsulation by Peter Black) you either rang the bell and knew it would be answered, or heard the bell and

Vera Zorina as a Hollywood star, *c.* 1937.
Edward James Foundation

Ruth Ford, by Tchelitchew, 1937. The hands spell her name in sign language. *Robin Constable*

Edward snapped in front of a portrait in the making
which neatly enshrines his earlier years in
California. It is of Gerald Heard, the guru who first
attracted him there. The painter was Don Bachardy,
lifelong companion of another friend of that time,
Christopher Isherwood, *c*. 1943.
Edward James Foundation

Mexico: the building on the Plaza Don Eduardo which served as the gatehouse to Edward's amazing jungleful of unfinished palaces, *c.* 1975. It also contained the only rooms ever to be inhabited.

Los Posas: Edward photographed by the side of one of his
jungle pools, sitting on a pile of bricks on the right, *c.* 1975.

Edward with his guacamaya, 1977. *Philip Purser*

Edward James outside his jungle home, 1977. *Philip Purser*

Poeted: Edward lies buried in the arboretum at West Dean, watched over by a stone muse, under this slab of Cumbrian slate. *Richard Ault*

answered it. He had been brought up in a society in which servants were servants, and though he professed to like American-style democracy, he was never adept at its give and take between employer and employee, or for that matter between customer and waiter. When a *maître d'* was once less than welcoming, Edward turned on his heel and never returned to that restaurant; but if after a prolonged absence they remembered him at The Beachcomber's (a Tahitian restaurant) and brought out his personal chop-sticks, he was inordinately pleased.

He was also, of course, the product of a society which had considered it perfectly acceptable, indeed desirable, never to do any work. People remembered from that period what he retained to the end of his days, the long domed fingernails which are in *The Forsyte Saga* the requisite sign of a gentleman who has never had to do a menial task. What more than anything else turned Edward against Hollywood in the end was that it was increasingly a town that measured you (in the local phrase) by your credits. Everyone he mixed with was either a writer or director or designer or composer or player, or aspirant to one of these trades. Even Aldous Huxley had been on MGM's and Fox's payrolls in the early years, clocking in along the writers' corridor for a daily stint on *Pride and Prejudice* or *Jane Eyre*. Christopher Isherwood worked on screenplay after screenplay, besides his books. The actors and actresses joined together in semi-professional stage companies when they had no work in the studios. The sculptors and the potters augmented their income with teaching at UCLA. Edward's name was on no one's payroll.

He scratched away intermittently, furiously, at novels which never got finished, at poems which were perhaps finished, but he couldn't be quite sure; he might want to revise then. So although a few were mimeographed and circulated to friends, and one or two expensively printed as one-offs, the bulk of them stayed set in type at a Los Angeles press awaiting an *imprimatur* that never came, until in 1976 the printer despairingly broke up the formes. Edward concocted a new pseudonym, perhaps conscious of the fact that he was talking away too much of his energy. He called himself Edward Silence. 'Edward James,' he addressed his friends, 'was a talking, talkative old piece of silver, but Edward Silence shall be pure gold. Just wait until he really gets on the gold standard!'

21

It is only fair to record that Edward was also remembered in Los Angeles with great affection. 'He was fascinating, eccentric and possibly the greatest raconteur I have ever known,' said one of his cronies from then. 'He could be a monstrous son of a bitch but equally he could be charming and hilarious.' Stories abound that reflect him in an innocent, Candide-like role, such as the occasion when he democratically tried out the local launderette he'd heard about. He took along his bundle of Turnbull & Asser shirts, read the instructions carefully, loaded the machine, set it going and – bored by watching the drum go round – went away to write a poem or have a drink or stir up a friend on the telephone. By the time he got back somebody had tired of waiting for a free machine while one stood idle and had dumped Edward's finished wash on the floor. Edward recharged another machine, set it going and wandered off again. When he returned the next time, the same thing had happened. And so it went on, through a long night, until Edward finally found his much-washed washing intact and was able to assume its cleanliness.

Gustave Field, the screenwriter, remembers going to a party at Edward's house and treading on something in the closet while hanging his coat. It turned out to be a Dalí canvas. 'Oh, is that where it was?' Edward said. 'I'd been wondering.' Another time he arrived at the house and found the whole place smelling of steamy perfume like a high-class brothel. In the kitchen Edward was boiling up a saucepan-full of old paper-clips which he had economically hoarded when they arrived on bills and other documents but felt impelled to sterilize before he could reuse. To enhance the process he had tipped in a bottle of eau-de-Cologne.

Daphne Moore, now Mrs Gustave Field, recalls an occasion when Iris Tree was living in an isolated log-cabin in the brush. She was entertaining friends with a sustained impression of Edward James when Edward James walked in. How he happened to choose that moment to drop by unannounced remains a mystery, but what impressed all present at the time was the touching eagerness on Edward's part to join in the joke without knowing what the joke was. Everyone remembers stories of his decision to investigate a nudist convention (this dates itself; it must have been still in the 1940s) and how the first morning he nerved himself, descended the stairs stark naked and threw open the breakfast-room door only to find everyone else fully clothed; when nudity was general, later in the day, Edward now perversely carried a box of tissues and insisted on spreading one on the chair before he lowered his bottom on to it. Safely home again, he reported to his friends that the most inspiring moment was when the assembled nudists stood to sing 'My Country, 'Tis of Thee' and then sat down together to what, said Edward, sounded like spontaneous applause.

His prowess as a story-teller was such that, according to the film director James Bridges, you felt you ought to be paying admission to hear him. He was at his best in a restaurant, holding forth to a party of six or eight. Though many of the stories concerned ancient relatives or London society battleaxes totally unknown to his audience, he always brought each to life with a thumbnail sketch, like a novelist introducing a new character. The same stories continued to figure in his repertoire, except that in the last years they became perhaps even more polished, more worked-over. The handiest idea of Edward's style as a raconteur, with plentiful imitations of fluting grand-dame voices, could be conveyed by saying he sounded not unlike Peter Ustinov in full flow.

There was the saga of Uncle Charlie (on his mother's side), who gambled away his Scottish estate at Monte Carlo and tried to restore his fortunes as an inventor, only most of the things he invented turned out to have been invented already, and more successfully, such as colour photography or the safety pin. His most promising device was a collar-stud which couldn't be lost, a problem so constant with the middle and upper classes of the day that it inspired half the cartoons in *Punch*. Uncle Charlie's stud had a built-in device so that if it dropped on the floor while being used it would emit a tell-tale *peep-peep*. Unfortunately he forgot to wind up the prototype and on his way to the Patent Office dropped it in the taxi and couldn't find it again. There was Aunt Olive, who although blind and nearly deaf in later life insisted still on being taken on long voyages, until her despairing grandchildren rented the apartment next to their own in New York, installed a rocking bed and a second-hand wind machine from Warner Brothers and transported the old lady wherever her fancy dictated, even – with the aid of a vaulting horse bought from a gymnasium and a few handfuls of sand tossed into the wind – to Timbuctoo. Among those who heard this one in Hollywood was the novelist Gavin Lambert, who adapted it for one of his stories in *Slide Area*.

There was cousin Dorothy (Dorothy Brett the painter) who lived in a shack in New Mexico and wove her own clothing and, burned by the sun, did look rather Indian. While minding the local store to oblige the storekeeper one day, she dozed off and found herself being studied by four earnest travellers. 'Excuse me,' said one of them, 'we were wondering if you were a Navajo, Cherokee or Pueblo squaw.' Cousin Dorothy replied, 'I'm just an impoverished English gentlewoman,' and went back to sleep. There was sister Sylvia in Laguna Beach who trained her pet mynah birds to say, 'Anyone like to play golf, anyone like to play golf?' so that when her house caught on fire once and the fire-brigade came hammering on the door, all they heard was a chorus of alarmed voices inviting them to eighteen holes. There was Mrs Patrick Campbell, whom Edward had known in her last, rather sad days in New York, when her only companion was the little dog she used to take to the park twice a day by cab. Once she cut things too fine and the dog disgraced itself in the cab. The driver, astonished as well as horrified, said, 'Gee, lady, did the little dog do all *that*?' 'No,' said Mrs Pat firmly, 'I did.'

It was not all anecdotage. Edward was also a fund of recherché information gleaned from books and gossip. A chance remark would set off speculation about, say, celebrities who had doctored their names. Henri Sauguet the composer was really 'Auguste', but for some reason he rearranged the letters, while Darius Milhaud – he once heard suggested – started out in life as Marius Dilhaud, which was less distinguished but really much more likely, he being from Marseilles and Marius a favourite Marseillais name, as in the Marcel Pagnol plays. This would lead to a story about the Milhauds in Hollywood and a return to the Ustinov vein to recount, with shrill impersonations, how they wished to impress the Stravinskys and asked them to a grand dinner. Everything went well until the coffee grounds from the sink blocked the drains, making it impossible to use any of the plumbing. Ordinary measures proved ineffective and in the end a special squad had to be summoned to dig out the drain where it crossed the lawn. And, Mme Stravinsky confided to her friends afterwards, the poor things had *kilomètres* of coffee. By association of ideas he might next have taken a swipe as Georges Auric, from whom he had commissioned music that was never delivered and whose wife's diary he happened to see. The entry read, 'M. Edward James est arrivé avec son Rolls-Royce, son Duesenberg et, espérons, son cheque-book.' How he 'happened' to see the diary was one of those incidentals best brushed aside, along with the sneaking suspicion that Edward James did rather invite such responses with his habit of trying to prop up his verses by buying fashionable composers to set them to music. It was in California, around 1952, that he received a historic rebuff, when Christopher Isherwood undertook on his behalf to proposition Benjamin Britten. Edward had written a little Easter hymn he wanted setting; he later said that Isherwood's letter to the composer was too cursory. At all events, Britten unconsciously echoed the E. C. Bentley clerihew about Wren ('If anyone calls, say I'm designing St Paul's') to decline the honour. He was, he explained, too busy composing *Gloriana* for Her Majesty's coming coronation.

In other arts Edward's patronage was still appreciated. He continued to buy pictures and sculpture, both in California and elsewhere, and he bought for cash, always helpful to the young artist. But perhaps his most significant gesture, in the light of later undertakings, was his championship of the Watts Towers. These strange and beautiful structures in the poorest immigrant quarter of Los Angeles were the work of a tile-setter, originally from Rome, called Simon Rodia.

For thirty-three years he spent his spare time collecting miscellaneous junk, from old iron and tin-cans and broken bottles to sea-shells and surplus tiles, and – unmoved by the jeers of neighbours – building it into decorative spires and pinnacles, until suddenly he vanished from Watts in 1954, and when tracked down in another town expressed no further interest in his handiwork. Apart from vandalism the towers were threatened by the Los Angeles municipal building department, which declared them unsafe. Edward was prominent in a campaign in the early 1960s to preserve a striking example of naïf art, and helped organize a public 'pull test' to prove the structures were sound. Old Rodia had used home-made cement and improvised chicken-wire reinforcing underneath his multi-coloured, multi-textured cladding, but he had welded large chunks of scrap steel into the armature; his towers withstood every test and are still there today, a tourist attraction.

Edward had also helped a couple of painters by installing them in the house at Milner Road. There is a story, indeed, that it was because they wouldn't move out again that he started his habit of living in hotel rooms and eventually parted with Milner Road altogether. He bought a house by the ocean at 31833 Sea Level Drive, Trancas, towards the westernmost limit of Malibu and therefore of the whole Los Angeles conurbation. How much time he actually spent there is uncertain. According to the playwright Jack Larson, Edward decided one night that the place was haunted and moved out there and then into a hotel. Edward hotly denied the story, while admitting with relish to other supernatural experiences, such as the West Dean vision, an encounter with his father's ghost on another occasion and a particularly gruesome manifestation in Cuernavaca, Mexico, which we will come to in due course. Whatever the cause, the Trancas house stayed shuttered and padlocked for maybe as long as eight years. Larson was with Edward when he first ventured inside again, and says it was like the *Marie Celeste*, with the remains of a meal on the table, dirty dishes in the sink, drawings on the walls, poems lying around. The only real damage was a film of rusty moisture covering the floors from a leaky tap. A day's work by a professional cleaning crew would have rehabilitated it, but Edward preferred to build a new house for his own use, behind the old one.

22

By 1963 Edward had decided to divest himself of West Dean. He was approaching sixty, without an heir, and had no wish to leave the ancestral estate – well, his father's and then his – to the tax man. Guided by his American lawyer, Robert Farmer, he set up a charitable educational trust to be called the Edward James Foundation. West Dean's thirteen tenant farms, its two villages, West Dean House and its contents, including the pictures, were all made over, together with other assets. There had been raids on the land over the years, to pay for Edward's education and other extravagances; the 10,000 acres were down to about 6,500. It still represented an endowment of some £10 million; nothing made Edward more indignant (and nearly everything made him quite indignant) than the assumption that it was all a tax fiddle. He could have become an American citizen, sold up and shifted the capital there – the money, after all, had come from America in the first place.

Exactly how the educational purpose of the Edward James Foundation should be realized was yet to be determined. Edward had long been impressed by a suggestion in Aldous Huxley's utopian treatise *Ends and Means* that future civilizations might consist of separate, self-sufficient communities like monasteries in the Middle Ages. The thought of dedicating West Dean to something like that attracted him. On one visit to England, he turned up at the Menuhins' house in Highgate to try and persuade Yehudi to set up his music school there. Menuhin had other plans, but more and more Edward was drawn to the idea of fostering arts and crafts that seemed to accord with the monastic ideal he had extracted (rather fancifully) from Huxley. The plan slowly evolved to make West Dean a college where skills such as book-binding and furniture restoration and calligraphy would not only be taught but also plied to practical ends.

Meanwhile the house itself was still let to Wispers; the business of making the dream come true remained mainly legal and financial, conducted – or rather, not conducted – by Edward at long range, in Los Angeles. Jack Larson, again, remembers going with him to the Beverly Hilton Hotel to help clear out a room Edward had occupied months before and had been paying for ever since. 'The walls were covered with letters and cables he'd Scotch-taped up, all marked URGENT or REPLY IMPERATIVE, all from lawyers and accountants and people involved in setting up the foundation, and when they got too much for him, scowling at him from the walls so that he couldn't work any more, he simply locked the door and moved out.'

Another vivid impression of Edward towards the end of his Californian sojourn came to me from William Emboden, a plant biologist who met him in 1964. It was at the West Los Angeles salon of an artistic neighbour, Kate Steinitz. Emboden, then a Ph.D student, had no idea who James might be. 'He was poorly dressed and without shoes! His enthusiasm for poetry led to a long evening, and I volunteered to take him home as he had no car. No one had mentioned his wealth. I assumed him to be a kindly eccentric gentleman. He indicated he was staying at a beach hotel in Santa Monica which is now the Synanon residence [a pioneering self-help centre for drug addicts]. When we came to the ocean he sniffed – it was low tide – and said the smell reminded him of Maureen O'Hara. He then told me that they had been intimate.

'In the lobby he discoursed on how the hotel resembled a ship with its prow jutting towards the Pacific, yet stranded. He said that his room was next to that of a former lion tamer who still dressed for the part and kept a mistress young enough to be his daughter. I did not see either of these people, if they existed. As I left, Edward asked me to join him a few days later. He picked me up in a very old car – a real wreck – and persuaded me to go collecting rents with him in Malibu. We stopped outside several houses while he went in. I still found his conversation fascinating. He would alternate between stories of being married to Tilly Losch and tales of how his sister was trying to poison him by putting oleander leaves in his salad. I still had no notion of his being a man of means. I did not believe that he really owned those Malibu properties, and while I enjoyed his stories of the famous people he had known, I didn't believe them either.'

A year later, in 1965, came a more worrying encounter. One evening Edward James called unexpectedly on Dr Emboden, as he now was, and said he was terribly hungry and would be grateful for any morsel of food. Emboden rustled up soup, salad and cheese, embarrassed that he had nothing more substantial to offer. At this point Edward 'became *very* friendly and made amorous suggestions'. Emboden, as ignorant till now of Edward's sexual orientations as he was of his circumstances, got the other side of the table. They circled round it a number of times before the misunderstanding was cleared up. Edward was downcast only a short while, and there was never any further trouble of this nature. Not long afterwards he invited Emboden to dinner at an expensive Santa Monica restaurant. William was worried as to how he would pay the bill, and envisaged the two of them doing the dishes, but at the end of the meal they left the restaurant without any transaction that he could see.

Finally Kate Steinitz told him of Edward's wealth and background, and when he mentioned 'the other little matter', said she had thought he could find that out for himself. Which brings us unavoidably, I guess, and at a rather suitable moment, when he was on the verge of a new life, to the question of exactly how Edward James was amorously disposed. Whether someone is heterosexual or homosexual, or both or neither, is these days not of great moment, perhaps. When Edward was growing up it could still be a cause of shame and subterfuge; undoubtedly the wreck of his marriage was attributable at least in part to Tilly's suspicion – or calculation, as he would have put it – that he was more interested in Hawaiian beach boys, Italian baritones and Oliver Messel than he was in her; it was with such accusations that she spiked her defence during the divorce.

Edward worshipped all beautiful things, he told me, including beautiful women and beautiful men. He had been a homophile throughout his adult life, that is, one who was attracted to other men, but he had never had physical relations with a man. In the reminiscences he had dictated only a few months earlier for *Swans Reflecting Elephants*, however, he confessed to having once 'given way' to homosexual advances, those of Nicholas Nabokov, composer brother of Vladimir, around the time of *Les Ballets 1933*. When you tot up all the little stories and take into account the quite openly man-to-man *amours* expressed in some of the poems, it seems likely that Edward was at least as homosexual as heterosexual.

23

Edward was spending longer and longer spells away from California. He had fallen in love with Mexico on his first mysterious visits in the early 1940s. He went again to stay with a school friend, Geoffrey Gilmore, who was running his Argentine meat business from Cuernavaca because he was *persona non grata* with the Perón government, and for a while Edward settled in this charming little cathedral city himself. When Gilmore felt able to return to Buenos Aires, Edward took over his house and its ghosts. Then there was Mexico City, where his favourite hotel was the old Majestic, because it allowed him to book in with his pet snakes and birds. But always he found himself drifting back towards the remote, unfashionable mountains he had so romantically discovered on that 1945 expedition with the Texan sergeant, and where two years later he bought a thousand hectares of steep jungle land. He would grow coffee and oranges and, above all, orchids. As manager he installed a friend and latter-day travelling companion, Plutarco Gastelum. Gastelum, a strikingly handsome young Mexican of part Indian blood, had been deputy manager of the telegraph service at Cuernavaca and the darling of the foreign community there because of his efficiency, not very common at that time in Mexico; nevertheless passed over for promotion, he was ready to try something new. He bought a house – or Edward bought it for him – in the nearest township of Xilitla, married and started to raise a family; increasingly it became Edward's home as well, and the family his family too.

Throughout the 1950s he was probably on balance still a Californian, always returning there sooner or later with fresh stories for his friends of how, to protect his horse from vampire bats, he had hung candles round its neck and the Mexicans thought he worshipped his horse as a god; or of the local witch and her scale of charges; or how, in an immensely long account, he had taken three pet boa constrictors with him to the Majestic Hotel in Mexico City and the mice he kept for their sustenance had escaped, and when an American woman along the corridor complained the hotel was overrun, the maid tactlessly said, 'Oh no, señora, they are not the hotel's mice, they are food for the snakes in the next room.'

By 1958 he was deep into bureaucratic muddles over residence permits and customs regulations: a plan to accompany Aldous Huxley and his new wife, Laura, to Brazil on an official invitation was frustrated, according to Edward, by functionaries who stopped him joining the plane at Mexico City. By 1960 he had concocted such elaborate problems of citizenship for himself that he cajoled

Jim Bridges and Jack Larson and a third man, Truman Brewster, into a farcical and almost certainly unnecessary attempt to smuggle him back into Mexico via the tourist-trap border town of Tijuana, just across from San Diego. They had just negotiated the American barrier without trouble when Edward suddenly leaped from the car and started running. They caught him, hauled him back into the car and safely passed through the Mexican side. Edward, not to be done out of his dramatics, contrived to miss his plane and keep his friends on edge with enigmatic phone calls and letters until at last he could no longer defer catching the perfectly uneventful Mexicana flight south.

Precisely when the balance tilted and he felt no longer at home in California is hard to determine. The death in November 1963 of the one man in Hollywood he unqualifiedly admired, Aldous Huxley, may have contributed. Edward had hoped that Huxley might become a trustee of the foundation he had unwittingly inspired. At all events, Edward continued to spend a part of every year in Hollywood or Malibu until about 1966, thereafter returned less and less frequently.

On one of his departures he entrusted the second house at Trancas, the one he had built in the backyard of the first, to a virtual stranger, a bar-tender he met literally on the way to the airport. Well, the house got looked after, at least until it caught fire and burned out. The original house remained shuttered until young Christopher Andrews, son of Oliver Andrews and Betty

Harford, enterprisingly wrote to Edward in Mexico and asked if he could live there in exchange for cleaning the place up and restoring it. He was still there when I drove out to see it in 1977, but the attorney Robert Farmer said both properties were due to be put on the market. I heard later that they had been sold.

I took the Pacific Coast Highway through Malibu, past the 'Colony' where the film stars of the 1930s built their beach houses, on past Point Dune to where the beach clubs and hamburger stands and gas stations finally petered out. Sea Level Drive proved to be a narrow turn-off tucked in by the side of another, private road. It led to a rough esplanade between the houses and the ocean. Chris Andrews said this was a fine surfing beach and, off the beaten track, one that still escaped the crowds of surf freaks who occupied other beaches from dawn to dusk.

The house was hemmed in by eucalyptus trees, cypresses and laurels, many of which Edward had planted. It had originally been a ghostly, silvery colour, but was now painted the dull red called barn red. A little novelty-store sign said 'Trespassers will be eaten' with a cartoon of a scowling dog. At road level there was only a garage or workshop. The living accommodation was one floor up, though – as usual in hilly Los Angeles – the ground rose so steeply that the other end of the same floor opened on to a scrubby lawn. Over the intervening slope Chris Andrews had built a timber deck. Inside, little remained of Edward's furniture and fittings: a table, the cobbled floor to a little entrance hall and passage: in the main room, a Franklin stove as invented by Benjamin Franklin and at this time probably the genuine old article, not the fashionable reproduction of a few years later. The old square sink in the kitchen, with its leaking tap, had been replaced by a double drainer. But it wasn't hard to imagine Edward there in the calm and stillness – save for the eternal roar of the surf – perhaps reading, perhaps working on a poem, resisting the impulse to go and see someone (after all it was twenty-five miles into the nearest part of town, at least as much in the opposite direction to Ojai), until suddenly the panic of loneliness would hit him and he'd reach for the telephone. 'Betty, could I come and see you . . .?' Was this another reason for finally settling in Mexico – the instinct that away from all possibility of calling up a friend the lonely man is, curiously, less lonely?

24

The leaves must now flutter from the calendar or, in a more contemporary cliché of the cinema to indicate the passing of time, a medley of newsreel clips bring us Vietnam, men on the moon and Nixon's departure from the White House. The 1960s turn into the 1970s. Edward is mostly in Mexico. On one trip to Europe he falls in love with the Portuguese Algarve, not yet despoiled, and buys land on which to build a home. Who knows? If that had come to pass, his last years and last deeds might have been very different. But visiting the site by car he accidentally runs over the dog of the military man who would have been his neighbour. There is a tremendous row, leading to lawsuits or threats of lawsuits, and the idea of living there is damned forever in Edward's eyes. Just as he had refused to set foot again in the house at Trancas after he thought it haunted, so he never returned to his land in Portugal, nor built on it. He simply left it as it was, until his executors sold the property after his death.

At West Dean there was both disappointment and consolation. Edward had long thought that the village lacked a focus; there was also a short-age of housing for estate workers; he hatched a scheme to build cottages in traditional Sussex brick and flint round a traditional village green which he would lay out just by the church. The local planning authority thought otherwise and turned down the application. But the way for West Dean College to go ahead was at last clear when the Wispers lease of the house itself ran out in 1969. Major-General Cyril Lloyd, a retired soldier of energy and imagination, was appointed to set up the establishment; it was he who determined the final form the college should take, with a strong emphasis on conservation. There would be work-shops devoted to the restoration of antique fur-niture and clocks as well as classes in folksier crafts such as weaving cane chair seats. The college would open, the general brashly declared, in 1971 – and in 1971 it did, if with only a handful of students.

With John Lowe succeeding Cyril Lloyd as principal, West Dean College steadily expanded. Within a few years it was reaching its then capacity of a hundred students, though many of these were on courses lasting only ten or five days or even one weekend. I have to admit that on my first visit I found it all rather Women's Institutish, and so apparently did its founder Edward, who was reported to have said he hadn't intended to divest himself of his family seat and fortune in order that housewives could learn basket-making. But he was proud of the two longer courses so far introduced, in furniture and clock restoration.

The Victoria and Albert Museum was already sending pieces to be repaired, he boasted, though he couldn't resist adding that so were Jewish antique dealers.

For nearly forty years by now, the name of Edward James had been out of currency. Few readers coming upon it in *Summoned by Bells* would have known whom Betjeman was singling out in his last lines. This anonymity was about to cease. The colour magazines of, first, the *Sunday Times* and then the *Sunday Telegraph* carried articles about him. The author of the latter piece, Patrick Boyle, whose family had connections with Edward's, was also making a television documentary about his chequered life and the jungle fastness in Mexico where he seemed to have settled.

At which point I can cease piecing together this story from Edward's and other people's accounts and start on my own. I had been asked if it would be possible to write a short biography of James (the original edition of this book), due to appear when the television programme went out the following year. I said I would need to meet him before I could give an answer. As it happened he was not very far away. He had taken to spending quite long periods in Ireland, out of the tax-man's reach but well placed for seeing friends, haranguing all at West Dean by telephone and generally stirring things up. He had also chosen to have two operations for kidney stones in Dublin. He always stayed at Leixlip Castle, just outside the city, as guest of the architectural writer Desmond Guinness, whose mother was Diana Mitford before she married into the Guinness family and Lady Mosley after she had divorced out of it again in order to marry Sir Oswald. Edward was very fond of Desmond and his companion, Penny Cuthbertson, despite – or perhaps because of – the nephewly link with Tom Mitford, who had treated him so shabbily over Tilly.

Edward met me at Dublin airport, the wary little bearded figure of so many reminiscences. Outside the terminal building a driver waited with a high, ugly four-wheel-drive vehicle of Japanese manufacture. We were taken the quite short distance to Leixlip Castle and the hospitable Desmond and Penny. They had only just said farewell to George Melly, writer and jazz-singer, who had spent four and half days recording Edward's reminiscences for the book that became *Swans Reflecting Elephants*, and doubtless entertaining the company between whiles with 'Good-time George' and other numbers from his repertoire. I couldn't help feeling like the man who comes round folding the deck-chairs after the show, but I got on well enough with Edward to be tempted to go ahead. Two months later I set off first for California, then on to Mexico.

25

Tampico was geographically the nearest airport, if not the best served. It also sounded the most interesting: the kind of steamy gulf port from where, in the songs of Brecht and Weill, the big black freighter would be sailing on the morning tide and meanwhile the sailors were drinking in the waterfront bars with their doomed, professional loves. It was certainly steamy. Stepping out of the plane was like stepping into a sauna. I hired a bright-red Chrysler Falcon, drove into town and spent the next three quarters of an hour trying to cross the sluggish river that more less encircles Tampico. I could see from the map the bridge I needed to take, but not how to defeat the traffic system and get to it. I kept finding myself in unmade one-way streets leading only to another shanty-town purlieu and then petering out.

At last, hot and sweaty, I was on my way. Out on the toll road to the interior with the slipstream blowing in the window, spirits revived. This was rich flat pasture land. Every so often there was the elaborate entrance gate to another ranch, the name picked out in wooden letters, and Mexican cowboys riding by, complete with curly-brimmed hats and leather chaps; and young boys on donkeys; and little stalls set up by the bus stops, selling beer, soft drinks and fruit.

Whether Edward would be there at the end of the road remained an anxiety until the last minute. He had said he would be back in Mexico towards the end of July, but Patrick Boyle had warned me that Edward's comings and goings were liable to be anything up to four weeks in arrears. As for telephoning to make sure, Edward himself had explained with relish how difficult it was to reach him at Xilitla, the remote hill town near his demesne. Spiders spun their webs between the telephone wires; the overnight dew collected on the webs and shorted the circuits. By the time the lines had dried out, he was up at the ranch; by the time he got back in the evening, the operator on the Xilitla switchboard had gone home. In fact I had failed in every attempt to get through, whether from England or the United States. Even a cable came back undelivered. So I drove all the way there now only to be given the tidings I was meant to have when I phoned. Ah yes! Mr James was away in San Luis Potosí. He had sent a message that I should go to the Covadonga Hotel at Kilometre 287 and take a room. He would telephone me there.

Kilometre 287 was about eighty kilometres back along the road by which I had just arrived, just outside the little town of Ciudad Valles where I had stopped for lunch. Wonderful! But when I had flogged back there, the Covadonga turned out to be a pleasant enough hacienda type of place with a pool just being refilled, and after I'd had a shower and a drink and dinner, and Edward had finally called to say where to meet him the next morning, which was at a completely different hotel not so very far away, I could reflect that at least I had been given an early introduction to the intricate arrangements and best intentions, forever going awry, of which Edward James's life was composed.

The rendezvous he proposed was a place called Taninul, where he had put up for the night on his way home from San Luis Potosí. Taninul turned out to be the set for a Mexican version of *Last Year in Marienbad*, a rambling, faded hotel in the middle of nowhere and at this time, in what was supposed to be the rainy season, almost deserted. Don Eduardo, as he liked to become in Mexico, was sitting at the only table in the dining room to be occupied, the remains of a meal, half breakfast, half lunch, before him. He hoped or, rather, assumed that the change of plan had been no trouble. The trip to San Luis, the state capital, had been a nuisance but unavoidable. One of his peons was suing in the courts for 120,000 pesos (then about £3,500) for wrongful dismissal. In truth the man had laid himself off, and ignored all attempts to coax him back. Don Eduardo was defending the case, if without much optimism, the law (as in England) tending to favour the worker, and doubly so when the employer was a gringo. Never mind, he had taken the opportunity while in San Luis to see about bringing electricity to the ranch with a view to setting up a canning plant, and by sheer good fortune had also happened to run into a young cannery manager who was going to come and advise him on other practicalities. Finally he had discharged a long-standing invitation to address a ladies lunch club in the town. He put on a shrill voice to imitate a questioner. 'Señor James, is it true that you keep gorillas as pets?' 'Not any more, dear señoras, and they were only little monkeys, not gorillas.'

While he talked I took the opportunity to register his appearance at this point in his life, a few days before his seventieth birthday. The hair so sleekly groomed in youthful photographs was now a tangled grey, the beard the same. The smooth patina of his skin, noticed by Ivan Moffat in California, had a weatherbeaten look, with the blotchy freckles of age. Nor, when he got up to lead the way outside, did he seem the manikin of so many reminiscences. He was rather a commanding figure, indeed a bit too much so, he intimated. Recuperating in Ireland after a couple of kidney-stone operations, he had put on more weight than he intended. He was wearing slacks and, despite the tropical feel to the weather, a knitted yellow sweater. His feet were bare save for flip-flops; one big toe was lopsidedly clenched – the deformity, together with all the operation scars, he variously blamed or thanked for keeping him out of the war.

Outside there were palms and bamboo trees and a big round pool basking in the sunlight. It looked inviting, but a faint whiff of sulphur in the air gave a hint of the surprise awaiting the innocent plunger: rising from a hot spring, the water was permanently at a temperature of eighty. Edward said that when his arthritis bothered him he would come and swim in it all night. He led the way over to the mouth of a cave in the side of the hill with a warning to look out for the lethal coral snakes, which liked this kind of place, though they wouldn't attack unless provoked. The last case in his area had been about ten years previously, when someone went to climb over a stone wall and actually put his hand on a coral snake. Twenty minutes was all you had if a coral snake bit you, as the poison circulated, so the man bravely asked his friends to chop the hand off. There was also what the locals called *el escorpión*, which in fact was not a scorpion at all, but a kind of slimy, scaleless brown lizard, and just to touch it was enough. Fortunately it was extremely rare, though he had seen one scuttling away only two weeks ago – it scared him stiff. In Xilitla before his time a peon lay down for a midday siesta; when his workmates tried to wake him he was dead; they rolled him over and imprinted on his shirt was the outline of the 'scorpion' he had accidentally squashed.

When he was relaxed, as now, his voice was pleasant and well-drilled, like an actor's or a preacher's. The patrician English accent was flattened by slight American intonations such as 'romance' with that short 'o' that Fred Astaire also used to give it when he sang 'A Fine Romance'. 'Mozart', on the other hand, became 'Morzart'. He

151

was, as they had insisted in California, a good story-teller, if sometimes an imaginative or a credulous one – I have to say that in his *Times Literary Supplement* review of the original version of this book, the late Maurice Richardson, who beside being a connoisseur of millionaire undergraduates fancied himself as a herpetologist, cast great scorn on these scorpion tales. *El escorpión*, he said, was obviously a myth.

A boy wandered by with an air-gun, intent on shooting one of the doves that fluttered about. Edward wished him, in idiomatic Spanish, poor aim. Now, where were we? Oh yes, the scorpion that was not a scorpion. He and Plutarco, his friend whom I would presently meet, found one in the house at Xilitla, where I was to stay, while it was being built. Plutarco killed the creature and was about to pick up the corpse and throw it out of a window aperture. Edward had to restrain him physically. 'It was still full of poison, but he wouldn't see that. Plutarco is one of those rational people. He was a bureaucrat before he came to me, and a bureaucrat may never believe in anything improbable.'

He went on to tell another story featuring Plutarco, and Plutarco's reluctance to accept the irrational, which is perhaps worth setting down just as he told it, to give a taste of his style and of the fussy but persuasive detail with which he embellished every anecdote.

'So of course he didn't believe in ghosts either. People who don't believe in ghosts are terribly smug about it. Poor Plutarco really had it coming

152

to him. I had this house in Cuernavaca. It was built in Cortés's time, in fact it was part of the palace of Cortés until they knocked down the wing that joined it to what's left of the palace. All the staircases and everything were very ancient and there were various stories of it being haunted. My friend Geoffrey Gilmore had the house before me and was very amused because his cook and housekeeper had had a man to exorcize the ghost, and the exorcist had come in with a little black bag and wearing a bowler hat and had gone up as if he was going to deliver a baby, and afterwards the ghost was still as active as ever. I never heard anything myself except the furniture creaking a lot, which you could put down to changes in temperature, but the architect John Rex and his wife, Elena, who came to stay while I was in California – I was supposed to join them here – left again before I could arrive, leaving a message, "This house is too full of ghosts."

'Anyway, Plutarco and his mother moved in – this was when he was leaving the telegraph service to come and work for me, and took the free lodging that went with the job. I was in my room, in my pyjamas, about to brush my teeth. It was just after midnight, and I hear this very heavy tread on the stone staircase coming up from the big living room downstairs. At first I thought it might be the gardener, who was also the night-watchman, coming to tell me that some Americans had turned up from California and couldn't find a hotel room and were going to ask me for a bed, which quite often happened. Or perhaps it was the

Rexes, back from Acapulco. But then I realized this was the tread of a very heavy man indeed, in the nature of two hundred pounds, and the gardener/night-watchman was a little old hunchback. It couldn't possibly be his tread. While I was adjusting myself to this surprise the heavy footsteps stopped just outside my door. I was within reach of the doorknob, so with toothbrush in my left hand I opened it with my right hand. Nobody there at all. Lights burning – electric lights – perfectly straight corridor. Nowhere anybody could hide. No niche, no cupboard. Just a rather narrow long corridor, with at the end a staircase going on up to a higher floor and left into Plutarco's bedroom. I put down my toothbrush and picked up a magazine and walked along to Plutarco's room and I said, "You don't believe in ghosts, do you?"

'"No, no. Naturalmente, non." Very pleased with himself, you know. Very smug about it. "No, of course I don't believe in ghosts. I'm not that kind of a fool." So I said, "Well, that's fine. You sleep in my bed and I'll sleep in this room." He'd been sitting up in bed reading *Reader's Digest* – it's called *Selecciones* in Spanish. He took it along with him, but evidently he was sleepy and though I'd left the window wide open with a full moon pouring in, and down below in the street – the Calle Galliana it was – one of those modern mercury lamps, he fell fast asleep. And I fell asleep too.

'About half an hour later my light was turned on and there was Plutarco, who was very dark-skinned – he is partly Yaqi Indian – looking

154

pistachio green with terror, and trembling. I said,
"What's the matter?" He couldn't speak at first.
Finally he sat down on the foot of my bed and said
he'd been woken by five voices all talking Spanish
– gruff men's voices – and a sixth voice begging for
mercy, saying, "Not that! Not that! Don't!"' – and
for good measure Edward added a few words of
Spanish in a high hysterical voice – 'and then a
noise of throttling, and someone saying, "Tighten
the cord." It was a man being garrotted at the foot
of the bed. Plutarco sat up, and not a sight of
anybody. He managed to get out of bed and,
moving *through* the voices and the cries of the
man they were murdering, got to my room. He'll
never never allow me to tell the story. I've tried
once or twice in his presence and he always shuts
me up. That comes of not believing in ghosts – you
get your come-uppance.' And he finished the story
as he finished almost every story, with a little,
reflective laugh.

26

From my original account of these days it seems
that I travelled with Edward to Xilitla; certainly I
remember him telling me in detail, with the
petulance back in his voice now, about the last
visitor he'd entertained in these parts, who had
insisted – against Edward's advice – on having the
shellfish when they dined in Tampico, and as a
result had gone down with a severe bout of
sickness and diarrhoea. 'He knew best, you see.'
Then there was a prolonged grumble about cars
brought on by the big yellow Nash we must have
been riding in. But in this case, where was my red
Falcon? Either I must have retrieved it later or I
now owe Avis five million pesos in rental.

Anyway, the Nash: Plutarco had bought it while
Edward was in Ireland and of course, it was quite
the wrong choice. Despite its size, he complained,
it was only averagely roomy inside, and far too
low-slung for the rough roads up to the ranch. In
Ireland, precisely the opposite had happened. The
West Dean estate had sent over a Toyota Land-
cruiser for his use, the one that took us to Leixlip
that time. Its giant elevation and four-wheel drive

were quite unnecessary for hacking round the outskirts of Dublin. This led to the sad story of the Range-Rover he had had shipped over to Tampico so that he could fly the flag for Britain with a vehicle ideal for his needs in every way; unfortunately, his first trip up to the United States had coincided with the introduction of exhaust-emission standards the Range-Rover hadn't yet been modified to meet. He left it at the border, flew on to California, then to Europe for a long stay, and by one of those combinations of miscommunication, misunderstanding and plain cussedness which everywhere lay in wait for Edward James, the desirable machine remained uncollected until the customs sold it to an eager Texan. The only consolation was that it was another Texan who bought a Lincoln Continental that Edward had to sell after a pet armadillo peed into the air-conditioning system. Whenever it was turned on, the car was filled with the peculiarly rank smell, Edward said, of this species' urine. He had often wondered what the poor man thought when the warm weather came.

There is a direct road from Tamuín, near Taninul, towards Xilitla: very narrow, rather rough and straight as an arrow across the plateau for sixty miles, but Edward had some errands in Ciudad Valles so we headed south, eventually, on the same main highway I had already taken. The orange groves and maize fields and clumps of walnut trees were lushly green under an intense blue sky with little cotton-wool clouds. Edward, in the course of a diatribe against officialdom in general and Mexican officialdom in particular, referred with sudden passion to 'this *beautiful country*'. Hills, then mountains, rose to the west. We were coming to the side-road which leads into this high ground. I had missed it first time and had to come back. Edward's driver Carmello – he was also Edward's builder, I learned later – was already slowing. Almost straight away the road started to climb in alpine zigzags. A new bridge crossed a fast-flowing river. The whole road was new, Edward said; before it was built there had been only an unsurfaced track and a ferry, which had helped preserve the attraction the region held for him, ever since he first found it in 1945. Another hairpin bend and suddenly there was this hook-shaped peak on the skyline, as distinctive as the Matterhorn or Table Mountain.

Huestmolotepl! The name, Edward explained, actually meant the mountain of the hook, or maybe the mountain of the needle. Only a steeple-jack could scale it? No, Plutarco and his son Plutarcito had done so once, on a two-day expedition. Xilitla (pronounced *Heelitla*) was the contraction of a much longer word, like those long Welsh place-names, meaning 'the place of the many snails where they strike gongs in the trees to make the bees swarm'. Or alternatively, I suggested, the place of the few telephones where the spiders spin webs between the wires to drive many callers to despair.

The first glimpse of Xilitla always reminded me of a little Italian or Spanish town huddled on a hilltop. Closer to, it was more straggling, with every kind of architecture in evidence from adobe huts through nondescript colonial to a weird and wonderful house surmounted by strange cupolas. The centre and also the summit was the little plaza with its fountain and obligatory statue to one or more revolutionary patriots, and the church and the bank and the post office and, on Sunday, a market.

Plutaco's house lay at the bottom of a steep, stepped *calle* leading down from the plaza. Predictably, it turned out to be the house with all the cupolas. An iron gate opened into a little courtyard traversed – the only obvious sign of Edward James's influence – by a path of raised cement feet, big toes prominent. Inside it was cool, with tiled floors, tall windows, arched doorways. The upper floors looked as if they had been added on at different times, as was in fact the case; two storeys, then three, finally these lantern-like gazebos, reached by circular iron staircases. There was a swimming pool to one side, a big play-room and a garage down at the lowest level. At the heart of the house was the kitchen, quite small, a dining room, a little television snug off it.

Plutarco was drinking coffee. In his late fifties he was still a good-looking man, with black hair brushed back from an Aztec profile, but since the early 1970s he had been suffering from Parkinson's Disease, and though Edward sent him to England for treatment with the new L-dopa drugs, he was no longer as active as he had been. Each year, he said ruefully, you realized that the previous year you could do just a little more. His wife Marina was a comely, good-humoured person, as doubtless she had to be, with five children growing up plus Edward intermittently a member of the household, not to mention anyone he might have invited to stay or those who simply turned up. Once a startled maid announced that Jesu Christ had arrived with twenty-five disciples. A self-appointed Messiah and contingent of followers from California had spun a globe, they explained, stuck in a pin and lo and behold! – it marked Xilitla. Edward uncharitably suspected that divine guidance on this occasion owed something to the fact that the Messiah had previously been patronized, before she tired of him, by his sister Sylvia in Laguna Beach. They camped on the flat roof of the garage until Marina issued an ultimatum: 'Either Jesu Christ goes or I do!'

Just now, though, there was only a young couple from Ireland, Patrick Guinness and his girlfriend Liz, and their baby Jasmine, the darling of the teenage daughters of the house and of the little maids who crept silently around like mice. She was born when Edward was in hospital in Ireland in the winter of 1976–7 having his operations for the removal of kidney stones. Her parents would take her to visit him, and he would tuck her in his bed and make much fuss of her, and, showing everyone the great scar on his belly, announce that it had been a Caesarean, of course, but father and daughter were doing well.

The routine of Plutarco's household was casual, at least when Edward was in residence, perhaps from long attunement to his unpredictable comings and goings. Meals appeared when enough people gathered together to have one, but there was always coffee on the stove and everyone raided the fridge for beer or Orangina. There was no air conditioning, by choice. It was in all the hotels because Americans demanded it; Edward shared the Mexican disdain of its noise and artificial, arid chill. Fifteen hundred feet above sea-level, Xilitla escaped the worst heat of the plain; the house was cool, even the cell-like little room at street level which I had been allocated. Every afternoon at three o'clock sharp, during the rainy season, there was supposed to be rain. This year it was proving unreliable, but today a token shower fell. Afterwards, with Patrick Guinness and Liz, I watched the vultures which roosted on the roof of the house across the street spreading their bedraggled wings to dry in the sun. Whose house was it? 'The bank manager's,' said Patrick smartly. 'The doctor's,' said Liz. A little way up the *calle*, towards the square, was a half-built house. It had been intended for Edward, as his own place, but over the years the idea was tacitly abandoned. It had stood half-built now since anyone could remember.

Prowling around Plutarco and Marina's one afternoon when everyone was out or dozing, I found myself in an elegant little drawing-room, evidently seldom used. On the walls hung pictures which could only have been Edward's – a Tchelit-chew, a Carlyle Brown and several paintings by the surrealist originally from Lancashire but long resident in Mexico City, Leonora Carrington.

161

Edward had known and admired her since the 1940s. 'Of course, for a long time she couldn't gain recognition,' he told me. 'She was swimming against the tide. She didn't paint abstract rubbish' – and he launched into a diatribe against abstract painters and the gullibility of the Californians who thronged the galleries on La Cienega Boulevard on Saturday nights to gawp at, or even buy, their meaningless handiwork, ending with a whimsical proposal that all abstract paintings should be boiled together in the hope that canvas and paint might melt into a synthetic material that could at least be used for making tents with bits of rather pretty colour in them.

Carrington in fact continued the powerful Gothic imagery of her mentor and lover Max Ernst. Here on the walls of the little parlour in Xilitla was a lovely, perilous dream of nuns sitting in a frail, storm-tossed boat with a bird-like prow while hungry sea monsters lay in wait. A strikingly simple, uncomplex study of a white bull against a green background was inscribed 'For Edward, Leonora, 1959'. I heard a story that in the early days of their acquaintance, when Leonora was penniless and trying to bring up young children, Edward had offered a derisory sum for two of her pictures. Despite her need, the painter flung the money back in his face. Edward was shamed, and from then on the friendship was firm. He even took a studio in Mexico City for a while and did some painting himself, under Carrington's influence if not her actual tuition. Some of the results were also hanging in the room: a fantastic lion crouching by the side of a feathered boy, or angel, in the depths of a luxuriant forest; an elongated, black-visaged knight astride some horned mount facing a creature with tiny Sphinx head, small breasts, long legs and hopelessly inadequate wings . . . And was it on these walls or back in Monkton that a calmer, better painting depicted that favourite refuge of Edward's dreams, the little city of Seclusia?

Certainly there in the parlour, mixed up with the neo-romantics and the surrealists, rubbing shoulders with Edward's weird beasts or standing on the shelves below Carrington's imperilled nuns, and somehow not in the least out of place, were treasures of a very different sort: a modern Christ, a conventional carved Madonna with gilt robe, photographs taken by Plutarco of Xilitla and Huestmolotepl, photographs of he and Marina and the children and Edward all on holiday in Spain. Because, for all eccentric touches Edward had bestowed on Calle Ocampo 105, it was still a bourgeois family house, and for Edward himself perhaps the nearest thing to a home he'd ever had.

27

Every morning Edward went off to what he called his ranch but which was which was really his playground. As soon as he could bully Carmello or someone into driving him there, he would clamber into the Nash, often before seven, sometimes still in his pyjamas and dressing gown. It would probably be dark before he came home again. I would follow a little later, out on the road that led back to the main highway but only as far as a wayside *cantina*, or shack selling beer and soft drinks, that stood at the junction with a rough, unsurfaced track. This was the old road Edward had spoken of, until quite recently the only road; even at a snail's pace with the drive held in first, any averagely sprung car lurched and yawed and sooner or later clanged silencer against rut. A spur off the track led into the property itself. Edward had found it when he was first exploring the area with Plutarco in the 1950s. He was looking for – well, he wasn't sure what he was looking for: somewhere secluded, somewhere beautiful, where he might stay and grow things. How he finally recognized this particular site as the right one had been worked up into a little story worthy of *Selecciones*.

Plutarco had had to go back to Cuernavaca and the telegraph office. Edward continued alone, with a sleeping bag. One night as it grew dark, the terrain seemed promising, untouched by civilization without being too remote from the links with civilization he always needed. When he awoke in the morning to the chattering, he thought, of a horde of women come to wash their clothes in the river, his hopes were dashed. Ah! But the sound proved to come not from the actual girls of the village but from flocks of parrots who had learned to imitate them. He knew then that he need look no farther.

The spur track debouched into a walled, paved square that Edward had modestly dubbed the Plaza Don Eduardo in the hope that one day it might have a bandstand and a lemonade stall and people would come from Xilitla on Sunday to enjoy themselves. And so they did, but not to listen to any band. They climbed up to the pools below the waterfalls to picnic and splash about in the water. Indeed, the local name for the property was Los Posas, 'The Pools'. The plaza was used chiefly as a car park. To the left lay the lowest and flattest part of the ranch; planted with banana trees and coffee bushes, it was also the part that came closest to earning that name. To the right the ground rose steeply and dramatically in a great piled-up vista of trees and intense green foliage dotted with the deep pink of the little flowers called *chicos* that grew everywhere. But what was

165

that curious building ascending from the edge of the plaza, merging into the trees and reappearing another storey or couple of storeys up, level after level, until finally it fizzled out in abandoned platforms and fat columns that had nothing to support? What was behind the strange red double doors, ten feet high but neither more than a foot wide, that opened on to the square?

The building was a glimpse of the concrete dream Edward was trying to realize in the jungle, the doors – if anyone could be found with a key to unlock them – were its formal entrance and a first intimation of its nature. 'Why do you make your doors so narrow?' asked the ladies of the San Luis lunch club, for they had been to see what Señor James was up to. 'To keep out fat people,' Edward replied, realizing a fraction of a second too late that he was addressing a uniformly well-fed sisterhood.

An archway nearby afforded an alternative entrance, with only a modest 'Private Property' sign to deter trespassers. A path led diagonally up the slope with, at the first hairpin, men at work on another half-built house. This one had – but it is pointless to itemize or try to locate in words all the strange constructions on this strangest of ranches; best to recall them at random, as in a dream. All were to Edward's designs on scraps of paper which his master carpenter transformed into wooden formes for the concrete. Walls were as thick as floors, floors as solid as rock. Fat columns rose to capitals decorated with massive yet oddly graceful petals. One or two had been finished in

166

coloured cement, while the rest were still plain porridge colour, and always the reinforcing bars were left sprouting from the end for the next stage, whenever the next stage might come. The only building that looked at all finished was the carpenter's shop, but this was due, some day, to be converted into an aviary. The carpenter would move into the half-completed structure he was to share with the coffee cleaning machinery, for the ranch was still vaguely in the business of growing coffee and sometimes its workers were actually diverted to this end. After the canning expert had been – the next day, he'd said – it might even be feasible to resume picking the oranges; at the moment that cost more than they fetched at the market.

Another aviary had a big bad-tempered guaca-maya (a species of macaw from South America) actually in residence. The plans in Edward's head called for its considerable enlargement, however, with flying buttresses supporting further storeys and little birds fluttering between the buttresses to create a kind of bird cathedral. Oh yes, and at the end there would be a house for armadillos, an armadillarium perhaps? The path that led on and up was meticulously laid in malachite and basalt chips, an idea Edward copied from a garden he saw in Granada; a wrought-iron gate in a stone wall was suddenly evocative of an English garden; the sun streaming through the wild papayas, castor oil trees, the jacarandas and hibiscus, the humming birds, the giant butterflies, re-established it in the tropics.

A flamingo occupied a small house with a pool. A second one was for ducks. A gate opened to a path through the little deer park, a patch of steep hillside enclosed completely by high stone walls; even in paradise, few of Edward's pets could roam free; if the coyotes and wild cats didn't get them, local hunters would. Out through another gate was the way up to the most ambitious of all the buildings, the House On Three Floors Which In Fact Will Have Five. This was to have been Edward's own jungle mansion. It grew out of the side of the valley, massive platforms already weathered by age, linked by flights of steps that, for all their solidity, seemed to defy gravity. The usual fat pillars awaited further developments. It required an effort to imagine the walls and windows into place, even more to visualize the inside furnished, but at least the view from the house was already there. In the cleft of the valley the river dropped fifty or sixty feet in the very model of a romantic waterfall – narrow, precipitate, musical – before swirling on into the first of the deep pools of Los Posas.

Down there, giant metallic blue and green dragonflies skimmed over the surface. There were also the giant butterflies, though not so many these days because of DDT, certainly not enough to clothe a sergeant. One yam-like column painted yellow, one still plain, rose to some purpose now forgotten, but another slender pillar was due one day to be topped by a fanciful duck house which no predator would be able to reach, Edward hoped, so in a sense the ducks would be free. Of course, there would have to be ladders up to the house at first, until they learned to fly up . . . On a concrete sluice guiding the stream onwards he had moulded a head of Beethoven, its nose and eyes now eroded by the water so that Beethoven looked more like a pre-Colombian carving.

At the head of the valley, reached by an increasingly difficult climb, lay *la presa* – the top – where the property opened out and Edward was trying to divert water from the river, by means of a dam of rocks and banana leaves, to supply an ornamental fountain somewhere below (he could have tapped a pipeline that supplied the next village, but since he had provided that link it would look more gracious not to) and was also busy planting wistaria and cypresses and amaryllis in an experiment to see if more temperate flora would thrive. The interest that brought him here originally was, after all, a horticultural one; it was only when a freak frost and snowfall in the winter of 1963 destroyed 18,000 orchids overnight that he started to build instead. He still kept a few acres of virgin jungle where no one had set foot for thirty years, and what it harboured was anyone's guess.

On the way down he said that he had overheard a group of peons holding a political meeting. One of them was telling the others that it was all wrong for a rich man to keep deer for his amusement, they should be killed to feed the poor. At this time he employed twenty men at 50 pesos a day, which worked out a about £10 a week apiece. The roll had been as high as forty workers, which made

169

him easily the chief employer in Xilitla. He was also a local benefactor whose good works ranged from a clinic to a St Francis of Assisi poem painted on a blank wall facing the convent. After thirty years he was an institution, the recipient of biennial vistations by the provincial governor and the bishop. But could he ever escape, altogether, the Mexican suspicion of the foreigner? Wasn't there still, among the locals, a faint latent resentment of this eccentric who had appointed himself their grandee?

That night, or another night, there was a noisy wedding party at Plutarco's house, with music and dancing and squeals from the girls as they tried to pin banknotes to the bridegroom's clothes. Neither he nor the bride were particular friends of the Gastelum family. It was simply that, as owners of the biggest house in the village, Edward explained, they had to give these parties every so often if they wanted to avoid trouble. It was a political occasion.

28

GOOD MORNING. I HAVE HAD TO GO TO
MEET THE MAN FROM SAN LOUIS ABOUT
THE NEW CANNING PLANT AT THE RANCH;
BUT CAN RECORD POEMS LATER TODAY. E.J.

Edward's notes were always in big block capitals,
usually of many different colours, but this morning
all were in red except for GOOD MORNING in grey
and his initials in black edged with yellow. With
the mis-spelling of San Luis it was maybe an
indication of an especially hurried departure,
extra anticipation of what the day would bring. I
couldn't help thinking that after thirty years'
acquaintance with Mexico and the Mexicans he
had remained a great optimist. No cannery man
arrived. When I found him he was busy super-
vising the mixing of the colour to make the
maroon cement with which one of the buttresses
of the bird cathedral was to be finished. Edward
watched intently as the peon stepped up on to the
bamboo scaffolding and started to apply the
cement. The effect was somehow different from
that of the patch already done; too dark, too red,

too blue, too something, so the man stirred in more powdered colour and then more cement and more water. Edward embarked upon a long story of how he had tried to build a duck pond at Monkton House coloured the same way, and how the foreman there refused to believe the process would work and, when finally persuaded to try it, mixed the colour with *all* the concrete so that it ended up only dimly tinted. The peon was patiently waiting with the revised mix. Edward approved and he resumed the application, a square inch or so carefully smeared on with a putty knife, then another . . . how long was it going to take? Anyway he'd only mixed one dollop, and would have to match the next lot all over again.

Midday found us down at the lowest part of the ranch, where the green coffee beans clustered on the bushes and yet another half-built aviary housed some Barbados pheasants. Edward said he called this structure his homage to Joan Miró because the colours and shapes echoed Miró's – his surrealist credentials, I suppose, exempted Miró from the scorn Edward otherwise lavished on abstract painters. Another bird-house, he said, was his homage to Max Ernst.

It was Edward's somewhat feudal habit to be plied with coffee and tortillas, at various times of day, by the wife of one or another of his trusties. He flopped into a chair outside the shack occupied by his foreman Fausto. Fausto's wife, latest baby tucked under her free arm, brought black coffee in big white china mugs. The tortillas were served as they were ready. On Edward's shoulder sat the big bad-tempered guacamaya from the aviary up the hill. He fed it bits of tortilla and let it drink from his mug and talked to it in Spanish. The carpenter arrived with a small problem. Edward drew him the detail of a finial on a scrap of paper and the carpenter nodded. 'You see! He understands at once what I want. In England he would think me mad.'

The guacamaya accompanied us when I drove Edward back in the evening – ah! I had still got my rented Chrysler after all. Poor Guaca, said Edward, he had lost his mate and was lonely. According to Konrad Lorenz, the species had the biggest brain-to-weight ratio after the dolphins. Macaws did not merely repeat things parrot fashion, they really understood what they were saying. This one made small harsh cries. In the dining room he perched on the back of a chair – one of a handsome set with high backs – and proceeded to gouge out thick splinters of wood and hide with his bill. Each bit of hide came away with a loud crack.

Edward's supper was brought in. He asked for a cob of green corn for the bird and, told there wasn't any, invented an instant proverb – a town which could not produce green corn was like a bath which could not hold water. Someone found one after all. The guacamaya tore into it, scattering bits everywhere, looking round with bright, truculent eyes. I thought it curious that someone celebrated for his fastidious cleanliness, who even now was dabbing away obsessively with a paper tissue, from a little stack of tissues, at every sign of spilled human food or drink around his place

– I thought it curious that he seemed not to mind this dreadful, dirty bird and its even dirtier habits. He said, 'I suppose I have been shat on by more birds than anyone.'

Patrick Guinness and Liz brought in Jasmine, bathed and freshly nappied for the night, and while she was there Edward's affection was transferred to her. Now I wondered if birds and animals and little children appealed so much to him because they didn't cheat him or sneer at him or take him for granted. Jasmine went off to bed. The guacamaya resumed the destruction of its chair. Edward gave it a tot of Rumpopo, sticky eggflip made with local rum, and took it to his room for the night. We hadn't got round to recording the poems I'd hoped to record, but there was always tomorrow.

The weekend brought the invasion of locals coming to swim in Los Posas and picnic by their side. Once the pools were inaccessible to all but the determined; then Plutarco built steps, a political decision again. Cars, a coach, two crimson juggernaut trucks empty save for the drivers and their friends and girls in the cabs, nosed up the track to park in the little plaza with much noise and smoke and the hiss of vacuum brakes. Cans of beer and baskets of food were carried up towards the distant cries of the bathers. Suddenly the whole future of this fairyland seemed very fragile. The Covadonga Hotel fifty miles away was already telling its visitors, mostly Americans, to go and see Señor James's follies. Where the gross red trucks had come from no one knew: something to do with the government, maybe.

Was some kind of Disneyland destined to arise in the jungle, with souvenir stalls and Snow White and the Seven Dwarfs (still cherished in Mexico as *Blanca Nieves y Los Siele Enanos*) grouped in plastic effigy? Or would the jungle, allied with Mexican lassitude, win the place back in the end? Already the colour was flaking off palaces which had only reached the first of three or five or even seven projected floors. The flowering trees grew up through the House On Three Floors Which In Fact Will Have Five. While Edward's enthusiasm switched daily from one focus to another, and fresh ideas came teeming, the coloured cement was spread on an inch or two at a time, perhaps a square yard by the end of the day. When he was away, nothing much happened at all. The picturesque half-built temples seemed doomed to sink directly into picturesque ruins, with no intervening period of actual useful life.

The afternoon rain was heavy. As night fell Edward came down from *la presa* by the long way round. The shorter, steeper path had been washed away and he would have been stuck halfway down if he hadn't been providentially rescued by a worker who had gone back to look for something he had lost. The pyjamas he had been wearing all day were streaked with mud. He was soaked through, he said, and would surely catch cold if he didn't soon have a hot mustard bath. He shouted irritably for Fausto to come and unlock the door to the Bamboo Cabin. The Bamboo Cabin was the very first thing Edward built here, and where he used to live all alone for days on end, many years ago. It was still there, but sentimentally incorporated into the house on the plaza with the thin red doors, at somewhere around the third level, along with a kitchen and a lavatory, and was almost the only room among all the buildings which had been fitted with a window and plastered within. He hunted for dry things but was distracted, characteristically, by noticing a poem written on bare plaster. It must have been there ten years at least. He shone the torch on it to try and read the words. ' "My house grows like the chamber'd nautilus" – well, that's right. That's a good image. This house has grown, bit by bit. "My house grows like the chamber'd nautilus; after the storm opens a larger room from my intenser childhood's sleeping place . . . where curled, my head to chest, I felt the grace . . . of the first need to grow. My house has wings and sometimes in the dead of night she sings." That's not bad, that's not bad at all.'

Outside, the great red juggernauts were preparing to leave, bright with chrome, exhaust chimneys as big as the funnels of a modest Atlantic liner. Trying to get away before them, I stalled the Chrysler and it wouldn't start again. The leading monster drew up behind us, the driver blasting his horn continually, implacably, until at last the engine fired again. Edward sat by my side without saying anything, without daring to show anger. Back at the house he ate hardly any supper, sipped a whisky, stared inertly at *Star Trek* (dubbed into Spanish) and *Miss Universe* live

176

from San Domingo on the television, too tired to climb to bed.

But next morning – next morning, Marina Gastelum was with many sighs and *tsks-tsks* unpeeling wodges of household receipts stuck messily together and spreading them out on the tablecloth to dry. It seemed that far from flaking out Edward had been seized with a new lease of life around midnight, and led his young visitors on a raid of the kitchen. In the course of concocting an elaborate hot drink he cracked the blender and it all ran into the kitchen drawer.

Up at the ranch he was as sprightly as ever. In the House On Three Floors Which Will In Fact Have Five – or Four, or Six – he showed me the palanquin by which he was transported around the estate when, twenty years before, a tree fell on him and damaged his back. Today, he was confident, the cannery man would turn up. Tomorrow he was going to be seventy. Through the flamboyanes and jacarandas and hibiscus his fantastic shapes and columns shimmered in the sun. It *was* enchanted, beautiful, a hanging garden of Xanadu. I found myself desperately hoping that it would still be touching some traveller's imagination (in this antique land) for centuries to come.

29

The first version of this book, *Where is He Now?* was published the following May. I had sent Edward a proof for his comments. He telephoned from somewhere a long way away with minor points and the tantalizing promise, never fulfilled, to tell me more about an aspect of the 1945 journey with the Texan sergeant which I had only surmised – the weird circumstance of their choosing to cross the New Mexican desert just as the Los Alamos atomic bomb test was being set up. His one other observation, relayed later via the agent at West Dean, was a modest disclaimer about his own paintings at Xilitla. He had done these solely for his own pleasure and relaxation. He had no pretensions about them and did not wish anyone to think he regarded himself as a good painter. Unfortunately, it arrived too late; the book was already being printed. After it came out, Edward was reported to be planning an action for damages – he certainly telephoned one firm of solicitors specializing in libel; they happened to be Quartet's legal advisers, and had to demur. Nothing more came of this threat; I gathered later that his indignation had nothing to do with his painting, nor with any other of the points he had raised, but was aroused by the Californian chapters. He thought I had gone behind his back in going to talk to people there about him. Since I had never made any secret of the diversion, and indeed gave him news of old acquaintances, I wondered if the real trouble wasn't that he wished to erase this whole period of his life when he had frittered away the most time with the least to show for it.

The transmission on British commercial television of Patrick Boyle's film *The Secret Life of Edward James* followed in July. It displayed Edward in his best raconteur flow, and its rather blobby surrealist titles were designed by the subject himself; but apparently he took against this too. It was the same, later on, with *Swans Reflecting Elephants*, and that was all his own words. Perhaps there was no pleasing Edward James. Whether he liked it or not, however, his name was now known to a wider circle than at any time since the divorce.

Meanwhile, back at the ranch, the Secret Life continued, if a little less secretly, a little more interruptedly, for another four or five years. Desmond and Penny Guinness, now married, went to visit Edward there and were straightaway witness to a brand-new Edward James animal saga in the making. He met them at the airport at Mexico City accompanied by a baby crocodile wrapped in a bath towel. Edward never liked direct journeys, and he particularly wanted to show these guests as much as possible of the Mexico he loved. As they zig-zagged their way from hotel to hotel on the way to Xilitla, the little creature would be popped into the jacuzzi to revive, but Desmond couldn't help noticing that it was steadily failing. In the end, Edward nursed it under his shirt until it died, whereupon he wrote a poem, 'An Ode to a Dying Crocodile', which he subsequently had set to music by the ever obliging Henri Sauguet, then in his eightieth year. The crocodile joins the sand crane in New York, the eagle and the wolf on the Palatine Hill, the boa-constrictors in Mexico City and the armadillo that corrupted the automobile air-conditioning system, in the bestiary that demonstrates Edward's love of birds, reptiles and animals but also that he could be cavalier in his care of them.

Desmond and Penny Guinness were up at Los Posas when a coach-load of American tourists arrived, delighted – as Desmond put it – to catch sight of the elusive Edward James and anxious to record the fact on film. '"Would you mind standing next to my wife, Mr James? It is Mr James, isn't it?" Edward looked down his nose and replied in his most gravelly English accent, "No speakee English! No speakee English!"' There was still no sign of a canning plant, but work continued desultorily on the jungle follies. Sometimes Edward would order bemused peons not even to mix the powdered colour with the cement but simply climb to the top of the building and let it spill to earth. He loved to watch the tiny specks of blue or red or yellow as they floated down in the sunlight. In Edward's absence, nothing at all now got done. Plutarco's illness increasingly restricted his movements and he could no longer keep an eye on the works. Edward was befriended by a young Mexican admirer, Luis Félix, who took over the management of the ranch until after a while he began to accompany Edward on the travels which took him for longer and longer spells to Europe.

It was in some ways a return of the same gradual disenchantment he had experienced in England in the 1930s and in California in the 1960s. He couldn't even have a good blazing row with poor Plutarco, the children were growing up and growing away.' Obliterating everything, Marina Gastelum contracted cancer, cast upon her as a spell – or so Plutarco believed – after a quarrel with a witch. She was the soul of the house; and for Edward, though in years she could have been his daughter, the loving, scolding, protective mother he had lacked in his childhood. The tumours spread swiftly. After she died in 1982, Edward never returned to Xilitla and the house in the Calle Ocampo.

Where he was now, mostly, was in France and Italy. The journalist Byron Rogers chanced upon him with a bevy of beach boys at a hotel in the hills above Cannes. 'There was this exquisite little figure, and all around him these bandy-legged gorillas playing exaggerated court.' A nicer picture of him comes from the sculptress Niki de Saint Phalle, who met him when Michael Schuyt brought Edward to her studio in Soisy sur École. 'I thought he was the most extraordinary elf, but

181

with great presence. He had a child-like quality, but also a twinkle in the eye. He was always very charming and courteous and never came by without a little present. I have only very nice memories of him.'

Schuyt had got to know Edward when he was researching his book *Fantastic Architecture*. He had rightly assumed that Edward might be interested in the outdoor fantasy, not so very different from his own jungle follies, which Niki and her husband Jean Tinguely were constructing in Italy. At Garavicchio in southern Tuscany they had turned an abandoned quarry into a garden to display twenty-two eccentric, outsize, colourful pieces of statuary corresponding to the cards of the Tarot pack. As big as houses, even as big as Edward's houses, the Magician, the High Priestess and the Tower bulge up through the trees. Fountains splash into the pool below. Edward, naturally, was delighted to find something so close in spirit to his own labours. 'As soon as he saw it,' Niki de Saint Phalle told me, 'he wanted to help!'

It was one of the friendships of his latter days he valued most, along with those of Luis Félix and Michael Schuyt and an Italian, Piero Boero, who ran a restaurant Edward liked very much in the village of Perinaldo, above San Remo. Then there were Desmond and Penny Guinness in Ireland. When they had to be away once he stayed with their cook instead, and was thoroughly spoiled.

Edward made what was to be his last visit to West Dean in the September 1982, for the funeral of a former secretary, Mona Heraud. In March of the following year he was in Paris, in April in Italy. In August he was in Spain, where he tried to visit Dalí. The old shocker was approaching his sad last period of illness and confusion, and through some misunderstanding, or so the artist's minders and hangers-on sought to explain subsequently, Edward was turned away from the house. In November he went to India with a great-nephew, Alexander Worthington (Xandra's grandson). Niki de Saint Phalle thought that he was becoming rather unhappy and restless. What had induced him to go 'racing round India', as she put it? It was almost as if he were seized with the need to fulfil every old unrealized ambition.

In Europe he somehow found, or appropriated, or created, one last fantastic abode. He had become so fond of the restaurant in Perinaldo that he moved in, characteristically taking up more and more room with his suitcases and papers and poems until the business of the place was being squeezed out. Edward's solution to this difficulty was simple: he would build his own apartment on to, or even on top of, the restaurant. Needless to say, this addition turned out to be no filmsy home extension, but very grand, lots of marble, quite a little palace. In the summer of 1984, not long before his seventy-seventh birthday, Edward set off for Paris in order to collect yet another cache of papers or poems he had left behind – contrary to the impression created by those stories of priceless paintings left in the loo, the Range Rover abandoned at the border, Edward always knew exactly where he had deposited what. Only the

183

perversity of the world and its timetables prevented him from reclaiming every item.

Whether he was harassed or impatient or frustrated on this expedition is not known, but in Paris he suffered a stroke and was taken to the American Hospital. He was partly paralysed, and in grisly fulfilment of the name he had once adopted in California, Edward Silence, he could no longer speak.

Desmond and Penny were among the friends who went to see him, twice. It was obviously very sad, Edward lying there unable to say anything. But he smiled a lot and Luis was wonderful, Desmond said, trying to jolly Edward into singing Mexican songs with him. 'If anyone could have brought Edward back to speech, it would have been Luis.' After some weeks he was moved to a nursing home in San Remo, near his last home. He died there on 2 December. His body was flown to England. The funeral was at West Dean Church, followed in the New Year by a memorial service in Chichester Cathedral. Edward was buried in a glade in the arboretum he had loved, under a slab of green Cumbrian slate. It is a very peaceful clearing, rather difficult to find unless you notice the small crosses carved into trees along the trail.

30

Among those settling down to watch *The Secret Life of Edward James* on television on 26 July 1978 was Peter Sarginson, who had that day arrived in West Dean to take over as principal of West Dean College. He was a little disconcerted to hear its founder say that he hadn't altogether intended to part with his fortune so that housewives might learn to make corn dollies or whatever. But in the early 1980s, Edward began to display renewed enthusiasm for his creation, and sought to steer more resources in its direction. It was self-supporting as far as everyday expenditure went. The need was for capital improvements, to the estate in general as well as the college. Already the foundation had discreetly raised a certain amount, with Edward's prickly approval, by selling off such assets as Binderton House, the *petit manoir* once occupied by Anthony Eden.

After Edward's death, the trustees cast around for further opportunities to convert one kind of capital asset into another, as West Dean's agent, Tim Heymann, likes to phrase it. Edward had left virtually all his remaining property to the Edward

James Foundation, including the pictures in his personal collection and the 500 acres of the West Dean estate, mostly woodland, that he had retained for himself. Selling off a house would buy a new post office and shop for the villagers, or the extension of the West Dean central heating system to the church. Disposing of pictures could realize enough to provide new workshops or student quarters. This strategy brought them into the very public world of art and property sales and, inevitably, the risk of being accused of breaking up a unique collection or selling off a national treasure.

Nothing stirred up such a storm as the sale of Monkton House and its contents in 1986. The foundation had considered turning it into a college residence, but it would have been a long hike for students quartered there. The idea of retaining it as a memorial or shrine to Edward was attractive, but again access would have been difficult and insurance costs prohibitive. Whatever the house was used for, it needed much spending on it if some of the flimsier embellishments were not to crumble away. Meanwhile it cost £30,000 a year just to keep it unused and shuttered. A private bidder was interested in the house and maybe some of its custom-made furnishings. The rest of the contents, especially the early nineteenth century curiosities that Edward had mixed with the Mae West sofas and the *Life* magazine wastebaskets, would have to be sold separately. 'It's all bugger's Regency,' one of the trustees was reported to have said consolingly.

Two preservation societies, Save Britain's

Heritage and the Thirties Society, campaigned to raise £1.6 million and buy Monkton together with all its contents as a unique fusion of 1930s décor and Edward's surrealist serendipity. The National Trust, *Country Life* and many individuals lent their support. English Heritage, the official historic buildings and monuments commission for England, agreed to try and acquire the building if the other two societies would raise the money to buy the contents. *The Secret Life of Edward James*, equipped with a new introduction by George Melly standing in front of Monkton, was shown again. For lovers of conspiracy theory there were newspaper stories hinting at skulduggery among the trustees. Noel Simon, the respected local author whom Edward had appointed as executive trustee, had abruptly resigned. His American attorney Robert Farmer was now chairman.

All in vain. Not enough money, in the end, was forthcoming. Monkton House went to Simon Draper of Richard Branson's Virgin music and aviation group, and the marquees were set up for a great three-day sale of the contents. In fact, the rarer items and all the pictures were kept aside for later sales in New York, while the majority of the lots that did go under the hammer came not from Monkton House at all but from the vast reservoir of bric-à-brac, stored in the cellars of West Dean House, that Edward had accumulated throughout his life.

I haven't been back to Monkton. I'm told that Mr Draper has spent a great deal on restoring the house as Edward ordered it, only with better materials. Even the woollen wall-covering has been replaced with more of the same. There are still a couple of yellow sofas of Edward's. The only major alteration the new owner has made is to extend the kitchen and turn the old servants' quarters into family space. Outside, he – or perhaps the great storm of 1987 – has thinned down the trees. At the time of the sale I thought it all a shame. But remembering the dead house I saw in 1977, I guess it was illogical to want to bring Monkton to life again as a tourist attraction while hoping that the jungle palaces of Xilitla would escape the same fate. And certainly the college has benefited from extra capital expenditure.

At West Dean House itself, one huge new workshop has been created by roofing over the stable yard; others from the imaginative conversion of the stable buildings, or within a newly built tower. All are warm, light and well-equipped. On all the long courses the teaching of the particular craft is tied up with the execution of practical contracts, so there is no risk – on for example, the three-year apprenticeship in stringed instrument manufacture – that the making of a lute will strike the student as a deliberately archaic exercise, like Morris dancing. The lute is being made because someone has ordered it. The tapestry studio wove twenty-three tapestries for Henry Moore between 1976 and 1987. Antique restoration courses last between one and three years, depending on the specialization. This can be in furniture, clocks, fine metals, ceramics and porcelain or the increasingly important field of reclaiming old and faded texts, documents and musical manuscripts.

The short courses are obviously still directed at the hobbyist, but much more sharply defined both in interest and the level of proficiency expected. A five-day flute class will be specifically limited to flautists of Grade V upwards; one course in making miniature furniture will be for beginners, another only for those with experience. Seven thousand students, according to Mr Sarginson, now go through the college every year, pursuing everything from life drawing to indigo dyeing. In the course of their courses they pick up an incidental bonus I spotted in 1977 and which is now officially recognized – a taste of the ambience of an Edwardian country house, or anyway an Edward Jamesian country house. To this end, much money has also been spent. Edward's dining room is now a conference room, the floor laid at last with the Neptune carpet he commissioned from Rex Whistler more than half a century ago but seems to have installed in Wimpole Street, where it couldn't possibly have fitted properly. It was found in the West Dean cellars and conforms exactly to the place where it is now, its one curved end fitting the apse-shaped end of the room, Neptune himself directly facing the old Neptune carvings on the fireplace.

Willie James's library, with its shelves of valuable but not very readable old volumes protected by ornamental grilles, is now a lecture room. A working library has been made from the old billiards room, but there's a snooker table in the games room. Mrs Willie's boudoir has become Peter Sarginson's un-office-like office, while Mrs Willie's likeness – together with those of little Xandra and Sylvia – may be seen below in a fine outdoor group, *circa* 1905, by Robert Brough, a painter of the school of Sargent who might have gone on to great things if he hadn't been killed in a rail crash. Other pictures on the walls include Tchelitchew's sibylline portrait of Edith Sitwell and two Bérards of – ah! – beautiful young men.

A wall-display Edward never thought of but might have approved is of weapons which Willie and Frank and Arthur James picked up on their travels in the Sudan. They came across a battle-field from the Mahdi uprising a year or two earlier, when General Gordon was famously slain in Khartoum. With the muniments is a framed sepia photograph of the brothers picnicking on the site, bottles of claret to hand. The Oak Hall with carvings designed by Rex Whistler and executed by the Englishes (an esteemed father and sons partnership) was the students' refectory in 1977; it is now much better cast as their club; in a particularly enlightened move, it also serves as a pub and social centre for West Dean villagers and estate workers. The new dining room sports a nice little hanging made by the tapestry studio from a postcard Edward dashed off to someone at West Dean in his last years, a Miró-ish design in bright felt-tip colours which the weavers have caught very well, and down in a corner the flags of his favourite countries, he said – Italy and Ireland.

It does seem a pleasant and useful place he

somehow set up. An Australian student doing the ceramics and porcelain course told me that when she finished and went home she would be one of the only two qualified restorers in Australia; the other one had also been to West Dean. As one of the trustees, Christopher Gibbs, once remarked, Edward always did the right thing in the end, if for the wrong reasons. Half close your eyes and it is still not too difficult to visualize him as a small, rather beautiful boy wandering through yawning rooms, a lone child in a grown-up world.

'Oh, but in all the photographs of Edward as a little boy he is smiling and happy! I think he liked to over-do his sad childhood stories.' Thus Mrs Diana Beresford, widow of an Oundle housemaster, still active in school affairs, a kind of Mrs Chips. She is one of a small corps of nieces and nephews, ranging in years now from early fifties to mid-seventies who, as Edward's closest remaining relations, maintain a bemused eye on what writers and journalists, and occasionally each other, are saying about their eccentric uncle. One or two have taken his surname, such as Angus James, who had a spell as Edward's secretary (what he remembers most is Edward never stopping for meals) and is now co-writing a newspaper strip cartoon. The last surviving sister was Sylvia, the one who lived in California and was supposed to have tried to poison Edward with oleander leaves in the salad. She used to like to ring up his lawyer Robert Farmer's office and chat for hours, just as Edward had done. She died in or about 1988.

Edward's Mexican property was left to Plutarco's

family and is managed these days by his son, young Plutarco or Plutarcito. Of the three daughters, two have married and one of them lives in Holland. Plutarco himself is housebound, but still enjoys company. The latest news I have at the time of finishing this book, in May 1990, comes from a recent visitor, the Earl of Mulgrave, and from acquaintances who have houses in Xilitla and spend some time of the year there – the English painter James Reeve, and the Americans Avery Danziger and his wife Leonore, who make films; indeed, are making one about Edward. It is provisionally called *Edward James: Legend Among the Legendary*.

Constantine Mulgrave came away with the impression that Plutarcito was puzzled as to what to do with the estate. Someone was keeping the paths clear, but all the animals and birds were gone. It was rather sad to go there, now that Edward was dead. The Danzigers said that the Mexican government had been making noises about taking over the estate as a tourist attraction, and, partly to head them off, Plutarcito was allowing conducted tours. Reeve brought the latest and rather alarming tit-bit of news: the house in the Calle Ocampo had been quite badly damaged in a bizarre and utterly Mexican incident; the man across the street had set off an enormous bomb in an attempt to murder his wife but had succeeded only in destroying his house and killing his child.

Conclusion

I have seen such beauty as one man has seldom
    seen;
therefore will I be grateful to die in this little
    room,
surrounded by the forests, the great green gloom
of the trees my only gloom – and the sound, the
    sound of green.

Here amid the warmth of the rain, what might
    have been
is resolved into the tenderness of a tall doom
who says: 'You did your best, rest – and after
    you the bloom
of what you loved and planted still will whisper
    what you mean.'

And the ghosts of the birds I loved will attend me
    each a friend;
like them shall I have flown beyond the realm of
    words.
You, through the trees, shall hear them, long
    after the end

calling me beyond the river. For the cries of
    birds
continue, as – defended by the cortège of their
    wings –
my soul among strange silences yet sings.

Edward did not, in the event, die in that little room
above the Plaza Eduardo, the only room in all his
jungle buildings ever to be windowed and doored
and lived in, and that not so often. But his poem
usefully brings us back to his last years and his
lingering ambition to be remembered, more than
for anything else, as a poet.

The thousands of verses he had written and
rewritten over the years were dispersed around
the world, some in letters he had sent to friends,
many others scribbled on scraps of paper found in
suitcases and drawers, some older ones neatly
typed and run off in the smudgy inks of long-
forgotten duplicating systems. Sometimes a stanza
from one poem would reappear in another; in
Chapter 9 I quoted some lines about Tilly I'd found
in a mimeographed sequence called *For the
Lonely*:

I do at moments think about her yet –
explain to me how one so like a child
could be so cruel, should be so false, so wild.
Believe me this: – she spun a kind of net
like some weird, magic spider with her charm
about more men than me.
                  She may still harm
my peace, unless you teach me to forget.

194

I let the quotation continue for a few more lines to let the poet confide to his new love that he or she did more loving, gentle things for him in an hour than Tilly – I assumed it was Tilly, but I suppose it could have been another – had managed in all their months together, and added that the next sonnet in the sequence (they weren't sonnets at all, but Edward called them that) made it clear that the new companion was a man. But in another poem altogether the seven lines above come at the end, to complete a perfectly respectable Shakespearian sonnet clearly addressed, since it is called 'O my tall nymph', to a woman:

> Oh my tall nymph! oh now that I have let
> you plumb this dark obsession in my spirit,
> you wish to gauge the quality of it –
> if passion still there be or mere regret.
> Not in my every silence do I fret;
> but since your love has caused me to admit
> what, for so long, I would not say – to wit,
> *I do at moments think about her yet* –
> explain to me how one so like a child
> could be so cruel, should be so false, so wild.
> Believe me this: she spun a kind of net
> like some weird, magic spider with her charm
> about more men than me. She still may harm
> my peace, unless you teach me to forget.

That version is one of the poems chosen for an anthology of Edward James's verse published by Weidenfeld & Nicolson in 1987, *The Heart and the Word*. It's a remarkably handsome book, with Rex

Whistler's design for the Neptune carpet on the jacket and, inside, the decorations he did for *The Next Volume*. I have to suppress the mean suspicion that Edward has reached out from the grave, chequebook in hand, to subsidize himself in print one last time. But the selection of poems made by Noel Simon, still his literary executor if no longer a trustee, is a revelation. Simon prints about 120, mostly from the author's middle and later years and all shorter rather than longer, because Edward was capable of epics of sixty pages or more.

There's a meditation aboard a transcontinental train halted in the desert while the track ahead is repaired, in mood somewhere between *Adlestrop* and the movie *Bad Day at Black Rock*. There are swipes at California and Hollywood in particular. There's a desperate love song to Tilly, printed immediately before 'O my tall nymph'. There's a reverential tribute to John Fitzgerald Kennedy written in the aftermath of the assassination. Next after that comes one to Evelyn Waugh that is joviality itself. And on page 73, under the title 'This Shell', I was delighted to find the final version of the poem Edward had read off the wall, by torchlight, in the same room above the plaza, the rain dripping from the trees all around:

My house grows like the chamber'd nautilus;
after a storm opens a larger room
from my intenser childhood's sleeping-place
where curled, my head to chest, I felt the grace
of the first need to grow. My house has wings

196

and sometimes, in the dead of night, she sings.

The shadows of the palm-leaves on the stone
have with jade evening fingers longer grown –
and now my house, by storms of sorrow bathed,
without is washed – so that the sinking sun
makes shine her desk, wide roof of words and
    pearl.
Deep house, your heart wants in the dusk to furl!

The deluge comes. The storm, still after me,
thirsts for my light. It strikes to swallow up
the flame of my identity. This house
is all assuaged and waiting for that sea
whose child I am; nor, thunder, do you cease;
but the high windows, drowned, break and
    drink peace.

When, back in England, I was trying to decipher it
from my notes, my wife liked it better than
anything else of Edward's she'd heard.

Just how good a poet was James? Maurice
Richardson thought he had only amateur status.
Edith Sitwell championed him in the letters
column of the *New Statesman* after Stephen
Spender's review of *The Bones of My Hand*. She
said that *invidia* had prompted the reviewer. In
California I met those who were quite certain that
one day he would be recognized as a genius.
Nearer home, his admirers are more cautious. A
young French critic, Didier Girard, is at work on a
study of the longer poems especially. He says that
he is not going to pretend that Edward James was

a major poet of the twentieth century, but he is quite sure he was one of the most interesting. The introduction to *The Heart and the Word* was contributed by Peter Levi, then professor of poetry at Oxford. 'I do not think Edward James could ever have been a great poet,' he concludes, 'but I hope he will be a starting point here and there for unexpected thoughts and pleasures, and will somehow survive as he deserves to survive, if only for his extraordinary and convincing love of life. The vocation of poet was central to him; it was the one thing about which he never wavered.'

Meanwhile the inscription on the slab of slate over his grave is uncompromising. 'EDWARD JAMES, POET', the letters spell. And who, looking back over his sad, soured, indomitable, surprising life, would grudge him the award? In death, he has at last been poeted. Here lies Poet Ed.

My sum

Most of my grief has been in the cities:
most of my joy has been in the field.
I am wooded around with fruitless pities
and trees of regret that will not yield.

Most of my tears were never risen
into the eyes and few were shed.
Most of my years sound like derision
with night scoff and whisper around my bed.

Fate from her balance gave me wealth
of farms and castles and field and hill . . .
then, with these, in her bitter stealth
she mixed in the blight of a sick weak will.

To this starved rich child, there might belong
not money only; that strains might come
Fate added even the gift of song:
yet love she gave not. That is my sum.

Index

207

211